NATIONAL
GEOGRAPHIC
KiDS

CAT BREED
GUIDE

A COMPLETE
REFERENCE
TO YOUR
**PURR-FECT
BEST
FRIEND**

Stephanie WARREN DRIMMER
& Dr. Gary WEITZMAN, D.V.M.
*President and CEO of the
San Diego Humane Society*

NATIONAL GEOGRAPHIC
WASHINGTON, D.C.

TABLE OF
CONTENTS

WHAT IS A CAT?

SHORTHAIRS . . . 26

LONGHAIRS . . . 168

OWNING A CAT . . . 254

FOREWORD

BY DR. GARY WEITZMAN

Cats are professional stalkers, hunters, and snugglers. They're some of the most mysterious creatures in the animal kingdom—and also among the most adaptable: From the fertile plains of the Serengeti to the arid deserts of Egypt and the humid rice fields of Asia, cats have evolved to fit into nearly every environment, ecosystem, and human habitation on the planet.

Think you know cats? I thought I knew cats backward and forward. I've worked with them my whole life. They've made me laugh, and sometimes cry, and I'm always astonished by their antics and behaviors. But until I worked on *National Geographic Kids Cat Breed Guide,* I didn't realize how many cat breeds, sizes, shapes, and behaviors there actually are! From the Abyssinian to the Singapura and Turkish Van, there are about 70 different breeds of cats on our planet. Though the domestic shorthair is the most common pet cat in the world, and the one we're probably all the most familiar with, you may see a reflection of many of these special breeds in every cat you come across. Buried in there somewhere may be an Egyptian mau or a Havana cat, or maybe a Peterbald or an ocicat. Never heard of these? Start flipping the pages.

Whether plain or fancy, cats are truly among the most lovable, and beloved, creatures on our planet. Read on and you'll be on your way to becoming a true international feline expert!

For those of us who love animals, cats are a huge part of what makes life worthwhile. Just ask any one of the millions of devoted cat owners out there. At my shelter, the San Diego Humane Society, we take in tens of thousands of cats every year— about a quarter of them kittens, many of them as young as three hours old. Even more impressive is that all those kittens come during kitten season, which runs from March to November. Our mission is to protect animals and ensure that every single cat and kitten finds a home. Taking great care of the cat you have, just as you would for any pet, is the most important thing you can do as an animal admirer and advocate.

OUR PURR-Y FRIENDS

The house cat, *Felis catus*, sits calmly in a sunny patch on the floor. Without warning, she leaps to her feet and bounces across the room with her ears flat against her head and a wild look in her eyes. She crouches, rump wiggling, eyes focused on an invisible enemy. Then—she pounces! Her imaginary prey vanquished, she walks serenely across the floor, her tail floating behind her.

Cats share our homes, but sometimes they seem more like tiny tigers than domesticated animals. Felines and humans have been friends for thousands of years. They're the most popular pets in the world—one in three American households includes a feline, and there are as many as 500 million cats living with humans worldwide.

Yet cats are still mostly mysterious creatures. Where did they come from? Why do they act the way they do? And what makes one cat different from another?

This book will answer all these questions and many more. We'll dive in to the story of how kitties went from forest-dwellers to couch potatoes, how ancient Egyptians worshipped cats as gods, and exactly what happens at a cat show. You'll read about amazing cat heroes, famous felines in film, and luxurious kitty accommodations. And if you're looking for a feline friend of your own, our profiles of every cat breed will help you choose the perfect pet for you and learn how to care for her, too. Let's leap into the paws-itively awesome world of cats!

WHISKERS TO TAIL

From the tips of their teeny noses to the tips of their furry tails, cats have unique traits that make them unlike any other creature on Earth.

CURLY COAT

BRISTLY COAT

COAT

A cat's coat can be smooth, bristly, curly, shaggy, fluffy, or anything in between. And some cats have no hair at all. A cat's coat depends on which breed it belongs to.

SHAGGY COAT

SIX-TOED PAW

TOES

Most cats have five toes on each front foot and four on each back foot, but some cats, called polydactyls, can have as many as eight extra toes total! Each toe is tipped with a sharp, hooked claw that can be retracted, or pulled up out of the way, when it's not needed for hunting, climbing, or fighting.

NOSE

A cat's nose is much more sensitive than a human's: Their sense of smell is 14 times better than ours! That super sniffer helps cats to identify each other when they meet and to detect prey like mice, who do their best to stay hidden from these powerful predators.

EARS

Using 20 muscles in each ear, cats can rotate them in different directions at the same time to pinpoint the source of a noise.

EYES

Special eye anatomy allows cats to practically see in the dark. On the flip side, cat vision isn't as strong during the daytime.

WHISKERS

They're not just for looks! Whiskers are a powerful sensory tool that detects changes in air currents to help cats find their way in the dark and locate prey.

TONGUE

A cat's tongue is an all-purpose tool. It can lap up liquids, scrape meat off bones, and even act as a hairbrush.

TEETH

At four months, kittens lose their baby teeth, and their adult set grows in. As carnivores, cats evolved to eat meat, so their teeth are sharp and knife-like.

CAT FAMILY TREE

The magnificent black-and-orange Bengal tiger spends its time hunting wild boar in the forests of Asia. It's nothing like a gentle, fluffy house cat ... or is it? Wild cats may be mightier than their domesticated cousins, but the two actually aren't so different. This cat family tree shows how the modern house cat got its wild side.

CARACAL

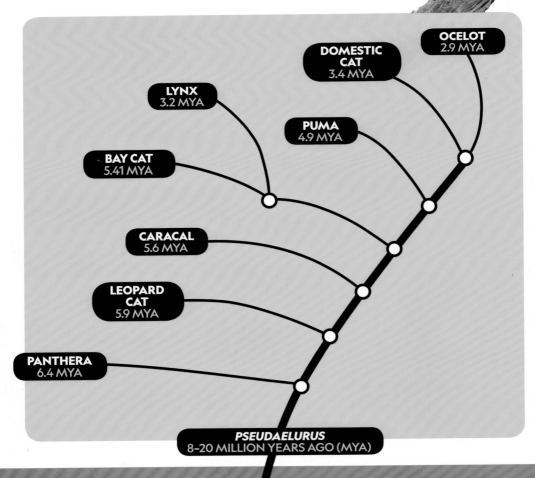

OCELOT
2.9 MYA

DOMESTIC CAT
3.4 MYA

LYNX
3.2 MYA

PUMA
4.9 MYA

BAY CAT
5.41 MYA

CARACAL
5.6 MYA

LEOPARD CAT
5.9 MYA

PANTHERA
6.4 MYA

PSEUDAELURUS
8–20 MILLION YEARS AGO (MYA)

PSEUDAELURUS

Scientists think the ancestor of all living cats walked Earth between 20 and 8 million years ago. This prehistoric feline, called *Pseudaelurus,* had a long, flexible back and front legs that were shorter than its hind legs. *Pseudaelurus* gave rise to domestic cats as well as the big cats, small wild cats, and the now-extinct saber-toothed cats.

PANTHERA

This group of cats includes lions, tigers, jaguars, leopards, and snow leopards, all of which have a flexible bone in their throat that allows them to roar. Clouded leopards are also in this group, but they don't roar.

LYNX

These cats, which make their homes across North America and Eurasia, have bobbed tails, black-tipped ears, and padded paws, which help them walk on snow.

ASIAN LEOPARD CAT

The most common small cat in Asia, this wild feline is about the size of a domestic cat.

PUMA

This group ranges from the tiny jaguarundi, weighing as little as six pounds (2.7 kg), to the African cheetah, a cat large enough to chase down a gazelle. They live in many habitats around the world.

DOMESTIC CAT

These small and furry critters are the house cats we know and love. More than 70 breeds snuggle on sofas and curl up in cardboard boxes worldwide.

CARACAL

These African cats include the tufted-eared caracal cat and the spotted serval.

OCELOT

Also known as the dwarf leopard, this group of cats lives across South America, Central America, and Mexico. They're sometimes spotted as far north as Arizona, U.S.A.

BAY CAT

This little-known and mysterious group of cats lives only in the forests of Southeast Asia.

FROM JUNGLE TO
COUCH

For a long time, experts believed that humans and cats first came together in ancient Egypt about 4,000 years ago.

Ancient Egyptians' tombs and temples are full of depictions of graceful, almond-eyed felines. It's clear that ancient Egyptians didn't only keep cats as pets; they also worshipped these animals. But new discoveries and genetic research have shaken up the picture, showing that cats became domesticated long before the time of ancient Egypt.

CAT'S CRADLE

In 2004, archaeologists found a gravesite on the Mediterranean island of Cyprus. There, a person and a pet cat had been buried together 9,500 years ago. Because Cyprus is an island, experts know that ancient people must have brought their kitties along with them on ships, meaning the cats must have already been domesticated when they came to the island.

Some experts believe humans and felines have been friends for about 12,000 years, since a time when humans were first beginning to farm in an area of the Middle East called the Fertile Crescent. People carefully prepared the earth, planted seeds, and tended to the plants. They harvested grains like wheat and stored their precious food to last them through winters when plants couldn't grow. But they had a pest problem. Mice and other small animals would invade the storehouses, eating up the food the people had grown for themselves. That all changed when rodent-eating cats strode onto the scene.

WILD AT HEART

Experts think that all of today's domestic cats descend from a Middle Eastern wildcat called *Felis silvestris*, meaning "cat of the woods." When the first *Felis* wandered out of the forest and into a human village, it discovered a buffet of rats and mice in the people's storehouses. It was happy to find this easily accessible food source—and the villagers were thrilled to have pest control. It was the beginning of a long and beautiful friendship.

their wild ancestors by only about one percent. But dogs, with their floppy ears, wagging tails, and splotchy coats, look very different from their wild cousins. That's not the same for cats: Today's house kitties have barely changed in appearance since they lived in the wilderness thousands of years ago. If you spotted an African wild cat in the forest alongside a house cat out for an adventure, you'd have a hard time telling the two apart.

But hold out a treat for a house cat, and you might make a new friend who will purr and rub its face against your hand. Do the same with a wild cat and you might end up as the treat. So what's the difference between lap cat Mr. Whiskers and his wild cousins? It's all in the genes.

TAMING TIGERS

When wild cats started coming into villages to hunt rodents, as early as 12,000 years ago, they were suddenly closer to humans than they ever had been before. Because cats hunt alone, they're antisocial by nature. But, just like humans, every cat is different. So some of the domestic cat's ancestors were a little less skittish around people than others. Perhaps these cats started hanging around campfires, looking for scraps. And maybe one of them finally ventured close enough to take a sliver of meat that a human held out for it.

Those friendlier cats would have gotten more food scraps. The extra food would have made them more likely to survive and have kittens. They would have passed their genes for a gentle temperament along to their babies, who would have grown up and continued to stick around humans. As these friendly cats crossed with each other and had more friendly kittens, the traits for curiosity and affection toward people would have gotten stronger. Eventually, this group of felines evolved very different personalities from wild felines. They were the first domesticated cats.

TIGER TO TABBY

When most ancient animals became domesticated, humans held the reins. We tamed cows for their milk and meat, sheep for their wool, and horses to ride and pull a plow. But we don't keep cats around to feed us or keep us warm—in fact, most house kitties seem to think we're around to serve *them!* So how did felines go from wild to mild?

Experts say that domestication had to have been the cats' idea. Wild cats began to live near human settlements so they could hunt the rodents that feasted on the food stores. That worked out well for the humans, but—as anyone who shares their home with a cat would agree—humans probably didn't coax these cats into performing pest control services. The cats moved in because they liked the easy life.

Domestic dogs are descended from wolf ancestors. Our canine buddies' DNA differs from that of

It wasn't just the genes for personality that changed as cats became domesticated. Though many wild cats and domestic cats look very similar from the outside, there are a few differences. Wild cats have slightly larger brains than their domestic cousins. They are also "hyper carnivores"—they can eat only meat. House cats, in contrast, have adapted to digest a small amount of plant material—likely because ancient humans' meal scraps would have included some plants. To make this possible, their intestines are slightly longer. Those changes happened over many generations, as domesticated cats' ancestors picked through humans' leftovers.

Still, there are some modern cat breeds that have retained some wild cat genes—like the Chausie (p. 66), which doesn't have the genetic adaptations that allow it to eat plants. Chausie owners have to feed these kitties special all-protein diets.

Scientists haven't yet discovered all the genetic changes that turned a wild cat into the kind that plays the piano in internet videos. But what they do know is that while people tamed other animals to help us survive, we became companions with cats just because we liked each other's company.

CATS CONQUER THE WORLD:
HOW DOMESTIC CATS SPREAD ACROSS THE GLOBE

As people—and the rats and mice that snacked on their stored food—left their homelands and set out for new corners of the globe, cats came along for the ride. In 2016, scientists sequenced DNA from the remains of more than 200 cats that lived long ago in Europe, the Middle East, and Africa. Here's what they learned about how cats left their original home in the Middle East.

NORTH AMERICA

SOUTH AMERICA

Scientists found cat remains at a Viking site in Germany dating to between the eighth and eleventh century A.D., suggesting that **CATS TRAVELED ON VIKING SHIPS.**

STEP 1

Cats became domesticated around the time when humans started farming, as long ago as 10,000 B.C. As early farmers started to venture away from the Middle East into new territories, their kitty sidekicks came along with them. Cats spread from there, reaching Europe as early as 4400 B.C.

STEP 2

Thousands of years later, the descendants of Egyptian cats spread across Eurasia and Africa. Experts think they probably hitched a ride on trade ships, where the pest predators were welcome stowaways. DNA evidence suggests that this might have happened as early as 400 B.C.

EUROPE

ASIA

STEP 3

By A.D. 1500, cats had become seasoned world travelers. They took long-distance sea voyages across oceans, traveling to the Americas and Australia.

AFRICA

CAT STEPS FOR CONQUERING THE WORLD

- Step 1
- Step 2
- Step 3
- Step 4

STEP 4

Over the next four centuries, people slowly spread across the globe, and their feline sidekicks went with them. By 1850, cats lived everywhere their human buddies could be found.

AUSTRALIA

UNDERSTANDING CAT BREEDS

Visit a cat show and you'll see that felines come in more shapes, sizes, and colors than you can count. These differences are due to their breed, the name for a type of domestic animal whose reproduction has been controlled to create offspring with specific features, from extra-fluffy tails to curly whiskers.

While most pet cats are of mixed ancestry and don't belong to an official breed, people who want a pedigreed (purebred) pet have many to choose from. Today, there are dozens of breeds officially recognized by cat registries.

A BREED APART

Cat breeding took off in the 19th century, after a national competition at London's Crystal Palace in 1871 showcased more than 150 exotic felines. As keeping and breeding cats became more popular, registries like the Cat Fanciers' Association began to keep track of the traits that define each breed. Today, breeders follow these "breed standards" closely to create cats that are perfect representatives of their kind.

ACT NATURAL

Some cat breeds came about naturally. These cats had natural characteristics, or adaptations, that helped them survive. Cats in Maine, U.S.A., for example, developed long, waterproof coats that helped them withstand the harsh winters there. Today, these cats are known as Maine coons (p. 200).

Other natural breeds came to be because they arose from small populations in remote, isolated locations. Long ago, one of the founding fathers or mothers of the Manx (p. 104) had a bobbed tail. A genetic mutation like the one that causes a bobbed tail rarely appears in a large population. But in a small one, like the founding population on the Isle of Man where the Manx originated, this trait can take over. The bobbed tail trait spread through the population, and today all Manx cats have one. This is called the founder effect.

MANX

DESIGNER GENES

Sometimes, breeders use the founder effect to help them create new breeds. With the help of careful crossings, a kitten born with a genetic mutation that gave it folded ears became the Scottish fold (p. 128). One born with shortened legs became the munchkin (p. 108).

Other breeds were created from scratch. The Bengal (p. 44) was born when one breeder crossed Asian leopard cats with domestic cats to create a new breed in the 1970s. Breeders use their knowledge of genetics to crossbreed one breed with another to produce kittens with the traits they want.

These "designer cats" are often popular pets that can sell for top dollar. But not everyone thinks breeding them is a good idea: Cats with wild ancestry can be dangerous, and creating breeds can result in cats with health problems.

GENETICS GAME

Cat characteristics, like a shortened tail, super-fluffy coat, or extra toes, are often the results of genes that are either dominant or recessive. A kitten needs to have only one copy of a dominant gene from either parent to be born with the trait. For example, if one parent carries the dominant gene for a striped tabby coat, all the kittens that inherit that gene will have striped tabby coats.

To be born with a trait carried by a recessive gene, a kitten needs to have a copy from each parent. The gene for the sphynx cat's (p. 146) hairlessness, for example, is recessive and must come from both parents to produce a hairless kitten.

Sometimes, inheriting two copies of a gene can be dangerous. That's the case with the dominant gene for folded ears in the Scottish fold (p. 128). Kittens who receive two copies of this gene suffer from a painful condition that

DOMINANT & RECESSIVE TRAITS

DOMINANT
The following are some examples of dominant traits, meaning only one copy of the gene has to be inherited for the trait to be present in the cat:

- Short hair
- Black hair
- Agouti (wild color)
- Color
- Striped tabby
- Extra toes (polydactyl)

POLYDACTYL

RECESSIVE
The following are some examples of recessive traits, meaning two copies of the gene must be inherited for the trait to be present in the cat:

- Long hair
- Chocolate hair
- Non-agouti
- White
- "Blotched" tabby
- Typical toes

LONG HAIR

WHITE HAIR

causes bone deformities. So breeders of the Scottish fold are careful to cross their folds with other breeds with normal ears, such as British shorthairs. This is called outcrossing. This prevents the kittens from receiving two copies of the fold gene.

WILD THINGS

Most animal species have different numbers of chromosomes, molecules that carry their genetic material. But domestic cats and many species of wild cats all have the same number of chromosomes: 38. That means that these species can be crossed with each other to produce new breeds. These crosses are called hybrids.

Hybrid crosses of domestic cats and small wild cats have become very popular for their exotic looks. The Savannah (p. 126)—a cross between a Siamese (p. 138) and a serval—has the large ears, long legs, and spotted coat of its wild parent.

Cat breeders are always trying to dream up the next popular cat breed. They try new crossings—like a wild caracal and a domestic cat, which produced an experimental breed called the caracat. It can take years for these new cats to be officially recognized by breed registries.

SIAMESE + SERVAL = SAVANNAH

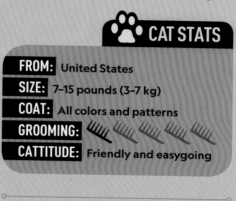

WHAT THE BOX MEANS

For each of the breed profiles in this book, you'll find a fact box with helpful information to help you decide if this is the cat for you.

CAT STATS

FROM: United States
SIZE: 7–15 pounds (3–7 kg)
COAT: All colors and patterns
GROOMING:
CATTITUDE: Friendly and easygoing

- **FROM:** Where the breed as we know it today was developed.

- **SIZE:** How big the cat will be when fully grown.

- **COAT:** The coat colors and patterns characteristic of this breed.

- **GROOMING:** How much effort it takes to care for the cat's coat. One comb means grooming about once a week; three combs means a few times a week; and five combs means daily grooming.

- **CATTITUDE:** Some cats are outgoing; others are reserved. Some love a cuddle, and others are more independent. Different breeds tend to share certain temperament traits. But all cats have their own unique personalities, and some may not fit the description of their breed.

CAT COLOR CHART

SOLID FAWN CAT

Some cats, like the Chartreux (p. 62) have only one coat color: blue-gray. But others, like the Persian (p. 220), have so many blends of colors and patterns that the combinations are practically endless. Here's a guide to cat coats, from solid to pointed, smoked, and ticked.

SOLID BLUE CAT

SOLID

Cats with solid coats have fur that is all one color, from ears to tail. There are both bolder colors (such as black) and softer, "dilute" versions of those colors (such as gray). Gray cats are often called "blue" in color.

COLORS
- ■ BLACK
- ■ RED
- ■ CHOCOLATE
- ■ CINNAMON

DILUTE COLORS
- ■ BLUE
- ■ CREAM
- ■ LILAC
- ■ FAWN

WHITE SPOTTING

Any cat with white on its coat got that way by inheriting one specific gene. Other genes control the amount of white that appears; it might just be a small patch under the chin, called a bib, or the cat can be totally white. Some white cats are albinos, a color caused when a certain gene is missing or damaged.

POINTED

"Pointed" cats have darker fur on their extremities—the face, ears, legs, and tail. This coloration is caused by a temperature-sensitive gene that causes the fur to grow in a darker shade on those cooler areas of the body.

TABBY

A tabby is any cat with a coat that has stripes, dots, lines, or swirls. Interestingly, all cats carry the tabby gene, but only some of them actually grow tabby coats!

MACKEREL TABBY CAT

CLASSIC   SPOTTED   MACKEREL   TICKED

TIPPED

Sometimes, only the tip of the hair is colored, and the rest is white or yellowish. How far the color extends down the hair changes the coat's appearance.

SHELL
Just the tip of the fur is pigmented

SHADED
Upper quarter of fur is pigmented

SMOKED
Upper half of fur is pigmented

PARTI

Parti-colored cats have two or more colors in their coats. Many breeds of cat, both shorthair and longhair, can be partis.

BICOLOR
Bicolor cats have solid areas of white and another color or pattern, such as red or tabby.

TRICOLOR/TORTIE
A tortoiseshell, or "tortie," is a black or chocolate female cat with patches of red on her coat.

CALICO
Calico cats are female cats with white patches, plus patches of black and red, blue and cream, or lilac and cream.

POINTED
Some parti-colored cats, such as torties, can also have a pointed pattern.

BICOLOR   TORTIE

CALICO   POINTED

CALICO CAT

SHORT-HAIRS

From domestic lap cats that like to cuddle up with you on the couch to wild cats that glide through the jungle on soundless paws, most cats on Earth have short coats. After all, their ancient ancestors didn't want long hair getting tangled on branches or catching the eye of predators. The first domestic kitties that gave up their lives in the wild to be humans' lifelong companions were shorthairs. The sleek look has been popular with cat lovers ever since.

ABYSSINIAN

The origins of the Abyssinian are full of mystery and legend. One tale says that Abyssinians trace their history back to the sacred cats worshipped by ancient Egyptians. And with their large ears and almond-shaped eyes, Abyssinians do look like the sculptures and paintings of cats found in the tombs and temples of ancient Egypt.

Another legend says the first Abyssinian was a cat named Zula. A British army officer stationed in Abyssinia (now called Ethiopia) in 1868 grew attached to the affectionate cat. He brought Zula home to live with him when he returned from the war. A drawing of Zula published in 1876 shows a cat with a coat similar to a modern Abyssinian's—but Zula's other characteristics don't match.

Only one thing is certain: The Abyssinian is a very old breed. Experts think breeders in the United Kingdom crossed tabby British shorthairs (p. 50) with another breed—probably an unusual, exotic cat. Modern genetic analysis suggests this mystery ancestor may have lived in northeastern India and parts of Southeast Asia. The new breed was shown in exhibitions in London in the 1870s.

Modern Abyssinians still have hints of their wild ancestor. With their muscular bodies, long tails, and alert eyes, they look a bit like tiny mountain lions. They have silky coats with "ticked" fur; an up-close look at the hairs show that they are banded with two different colors. Most have reddish brown coats, but they can also be a light tan "fawn" color, chocolate, or blue.

EYES RIMMED IN BLACK

CAT STATS

FROM: Abyssinia (now Ethiopia)
SIZE: 9–17 pounds (4–7.5 kg)
COAT: Ticked in brown, fawn, chocolate, and blue
GROOMING:
CATTITUDE: Social and intelligent

LARGE,
WIDE-SET
EARS

SILKY COAT

SLENDER
BODY

SLENDER LEGS

Like the wild cats they resemble, Abyssinians like to be up as high as possible. A tall cat tree makes for lots of good perches for this athletic breed to climb up to. Without one, you might find your Abyssinian on the highest shelf in your closet or on top of the refrigerator!

Without something to do, Abyssinians might search for their own entertainment—and can cause chaos in the house. Abyssinians need lots of stimulation to keep them content. If they live in a home where people are gone all day at work or school, they might need another cat to keep them company. Toys, playtime, and lots of human attention will help keep Abyssinians busy and happy.

Abyssinians—or "Abys"—as their owners affectionately call them, are highly intelligent and affectionate cats. They have a reputation for always wanting to be the center of attention. Your pet Aby might sit on your textbook while you're trying to study or playfully bat your fingers away from your keyboard. Only once you stop what you're doing and turn your attention to your Aby will he or she be content!

Many owners teach their active Abyssinians how to **FETCH A SMALL TOY!**

BROAD HEAD

TUFTED EARS

DENSE, MEDIUM-SHORT COAT

WIDE NOSE

WIDE, BOBBED TAIL

LARGE, ROUND PAWS

This breed may not have a long tail, but it has **NO SHORTAGE OF PERSONALITY.**

AMERICAN BOBTAIL
SHORTHAIR

American bobtails get their name from their short tails—but no two are the same. Some have straight tails; other tails are curved or kinked. Their distinctive "bobbed" appearance is the result of a natural genetic mutation.

There are bobtail cats all around the world, from Japan to the islands off of Spain and Portugal, where colonies of short-tailed cats have made their home for hundreds of years. But the American bobtail breed was born when American couple John and Brenda Saunders brought a mewing bobtail kitten home with them from a vacation to Arizona in the 1960s. They named him Yodi, and he became the father of the breed.

The Saunderses, along with help from a cat breeder friend, began a search for naturally short-tailed cats around the United States and Canada to cross with Yodi and then his offspring. The American bobtail was recognized as an official breed in 2002.

American bobtails were selected to have sweet tempers. Even though they look a little wild, with their tufted ears and powerful bodies, they are known to be easygoing cats who get along with people, kids, and other pets. They are good choices for rowdy households and will often join right in on the fun.

American bobtails are known to follow their owners around the house. They're not shy and will greet visitors—or even the mailman! Some owners say they have even trained their American bobtails to walk nicely on a leash. The American bobtail's calm and friendly personality also makes these cats good travelers. They're favorite companions of RV drivers and long-distance truckers, who cross America's open roads with their furry friends by their sides.

🐾 CAT STATS

FROM: United States
SIZE: 7–15 pounds (3–7 kg)
COAT: All colors and patterns
GROOMING:
CATTITUDE: Friendly and easygoing

AMERICAN SHORTHAIR

When the *Mayflower* crossed the stormy Atlantic Ocean and finally docked at Plymouth, Massachusetts, in 1620, it wasn't just people who stepped onto land in the New World. Historians think cats came with them. The descendants of these seafaring felines are today's American shorthairs.

Cats were unofficial crewmembers on many ships; sailors loved having them along for the ride because they kept rats and mice out of the ship's food stores. On land, they performed the same task for farmers, shopkeepers, and homeowners. Tough, hardy, and good hunters, shorthairs were the perfect cat for the job. A publication from 1634 even credits them with saving one New England colony's crops from squirrels and chipmunks!

As settlers moved across the continent, they took their cats along. Shorthairs became the unofficial pest control of the Wild West. Eventually, they made their way into their owners' hearts—and into their homes. People began breeding American shorthairs around 1900, and the breed was officially recognized in the 1960s.

Today, most American shorthairs are family pets, not barnyard cats. But because they started out as rodent-hunters, they were bred to be hearty, strong, and healthy. They have thick coats to keep them warm

CAT STATS

FROM: United States

SIZE: 8–15 pounds (3.5–7 kg)

COAT: Most solid colors and shades, along with bicolor, tabby, and tortie

GROOMING:

CATTITUDE: Calm but moderately active

on long, cold nights spent stalking and pouncing outdoors. They have short, muscular legs, and powerful bodies: Pick one up and you'll feel that they're heavy for their size. American shorthairs can easily become overweight, so experts recommend keeping a close watch on their food intake.

These cats are calm enough to be good human companions but active enough to be the perfect playmate for kids. They generally get along well with other animals, too. However, they're not the cuddliest breed, preferring to lay close by your side instead of snuggling right in your lap. And even though they make sweet pets, if a rodent gets in the house, watch out! American shorthairs still have the hunting instinct of their adventurous ancestors.

Shorthairs were the **UNOFFICIAL PEST CONTROL** of the Wild West.

LARGE, WIDE, ROUNDED HEAD

SHORT, THICK COAT

ROUND PAWS

POWERFUL BODY

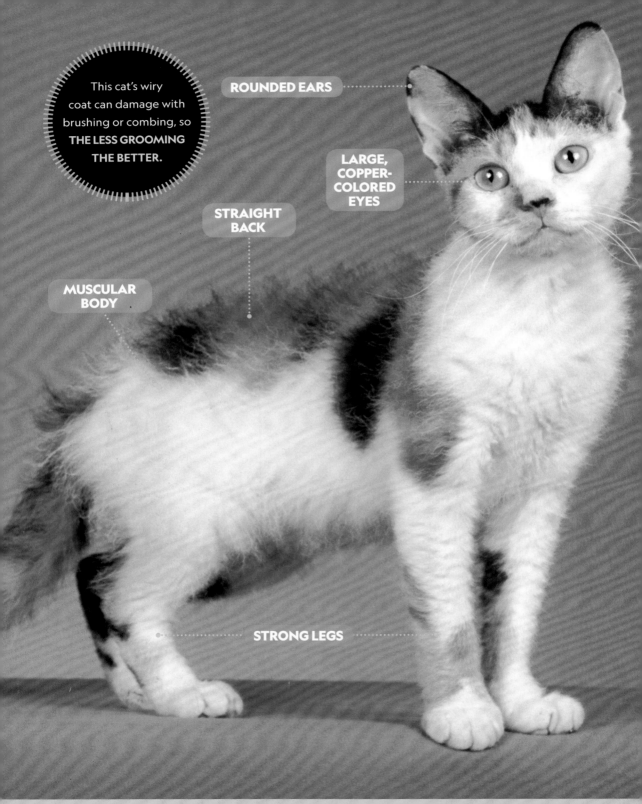

This cat's wiry coat can damage with brushing or combing, so **THE LESS GROOMING THE BETTER.**

ROUNDED EARS

LARGE, COPPER-COLORED EYES

STRAIGHT BACK

MUSCULAR BODY

STRONG LEGS

AMERICAN WIREHAIR

In 1966, a litter of kittens was born in New York State. Though both parents had average cat coats, one of the kittens had unusual wiry fur. A local cat breeder purchased the unique kitten for $50, and it became the founding member of a new breed called the American wirehair. The breeder set about crossing the kinky-haired kitty with American shorthairs to make more cats with unusual coats.

It's not unusual for kittens to be born with genetic mutations like the one that caused the American wirehair's kinked (or bent) coat. But usually, these mutations pop up in different cats all over the world. To this day, the one causing the wiry coat has only ever been seen in the United States.

Each hair of a wirehair cat's distinctive coat is crimped and bent. Even its whiskers are kinked! No two wirehairs' coats are precisely the same—their exact texture depends on the coats of their parents. Some cats have highly kinked hairs, whereas others' hairs may have a single bend, forming a hook at the end. Their coats are rough and springy to the touch; some people say they feel like steel wool.

Wirehairs are descendants of American shorthairs. But these cats are not just shorthairs with rough coats. As breeders brought up wirehair kittens, they noticed other unique traits, like high cheekbones and muscular legs. These cats were accepted as their own breed in 1978.

Personality-wise, the American wirehair has a lot in common with its shorthair cousin. They're not usually lap cats who need constant attention. But they do love their humans and will follow them from room to room, or snooze on the end of the bed. American wirehairs are good-natured, gentle cats who make great companions. They're good choices for families with children and dogs or other pets. And they're easy to care for: Because their crimped coats are brittle and can break easily, experts actually advise that American wirehairs should be groomed only when absolutely necessary.

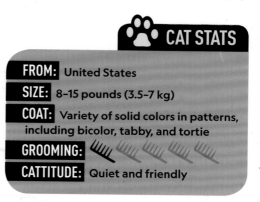

CAT STATS

FROM: United States

SIZE: 8–15 pounds (3.5–7 kg)

COAT: Variety of solid colors in patterns, including bicolor, tabby, and tortie

GROOMING:

CATTITUDE: Quiet and friendly

CAT SENSES

Your kitty might be a ball of fluff that loves to spend the day snoozing in a patch of sunlight. But on the inside, Fluffy is a fearless feline with quick reflexes and keen senses. That's because cats evolved, or changed slowly over millions of years, to be excellent hunters. Though most are house cats today, they still have all the hunting skills of their ancestors.

1

2

3

4

1. SHARP HEARING

Cats have excellent hearing: Their sensitive ears can detect noises human ears can't. Whereas humans can hear up to about 20,000 hertz—a unit of measure that tells a sound's pitch—cats can hear much higher-pitched noises, up to about 65,000 hertz. That helps them detect the squeaks of the rodents they like to eat. And their ears swivel independently like satellite dishes to help them capture sound. By moving their ears, cats can pinpoint exactly where the sound is coming from. Then—they pounce!

2. NIGHT VISION

Your domestic cat's wild ancestors hunted under the cover of darkness. Their eyes evolved to work best at night, which helped them sneak up on unsuspecting prey. Their night vision is extraordinary: Cats have between six and eight times more rods—the sensors that see in black and white, used for night vision—than humans do. Cats' eyes are also highly attuned to sensing movement due to better peripheral vision than ours, an ability that helps them track prey. Though they do see some colors, their eyes aren't as sharp as a human's in the daytime, and reds and greens probably look gray to them.

3. SUPER SNIFFER

A cat's sense of smell is much stronger than a human's. A human's nose has about five million olfactory receptors that sense odors—but some experts think a cat has as many as 200 million! Cats use their sense of smell to track down prey and also to process scent signals left by other cats. Cats even have a special organ in the roof of their mouths called the vomeronasal organ, mainly used for analyzing other cats' odors. Cats make a grimacing face as they use their tongues to flick scents toward this organ.

GLOWING EYES

Have you ever spotted a cat at night with a flashlight or a car's headlights? Then you might have noticed a pair of glowing golden eyes looking back at you. Cats have a special part of their eye called the *tapetum lucidum* that helps trap light, enhancing a cat's night vision. When a source of light strikes the tapetum lucidum at night, it appears as a glowing circle.

4. WIRED WHISKERS

Cats' whiskers aren't just for looks; they're highly sensitive touch organs. Technically called vibrissae, whiskers grow in tufts on either side of the nose, over the eyes, on the chin, and on the backs of the legs. Whiskers grow deep into the cat's skin, with lots of nerve endings at the base. The nerves allow the sensors to detect the movement of air around nearby obstacles. These sensitive sensors help a cat wind its way around living room furniture, even when the room is totally dark.

THE CAT
BRAIN

Dogs can be trained to guide the blind, sniff out dangerous substances, and even leap out of helicopters onto a battlefield. Cats, on the other hand, aren't exactly known for their trainability. But does that mean they're not so smart, or is there more going on inside their heads than we realize?

SMALL BUT MIGHTY

Cats' brains are relatively small for animals their size—about 0.9 percent of their body weight, compared with two percent for humans and 1.2 percent for dogs. But when it comes to intelligence, size isn't always the most important thing.

Experts say that the structure of the brain—and especially the amount of folds on its surface—is a better way to judge intelligence. The structure of a cat's brain is about 90 percent similar to a human's. And the folded shape of their cerebral cortex, the part of the brain involved in processing information, means that it can hold a lot of neurons, or brain cells—about 300 million, compared with about 160 million neurons in a dog's brain. (Compare that to about 84 billion neurons in our brains.) Hmm—maybe cats really do rule after all!

GETTING A SENSE

The areas of the brain that interpret information from the senses—like smell, hearing, and sight—are highly developed in the cat brain. Vision is the sense cats rely on most: They use it for seeking out, stalking, and hunting prey. The area of the cat brain that receives input from the eyes has more neurons than the equivalent area of the human brain!

The part of the brain that controls a cat's paws is highly developed, too. That gives cats the ability to use their paws almost like hands to grab and grip objects.

Cats even one-up people when it comes to finding their way around. The cat brain has a built-in compass that senses Earth's magnetic fields to help cats navigate. That may explain how some cats can find their way home after moving hundreds of miles away.

OLFACTORY BULB

FRONTAL LOBE (CEREBRUM)

TEMPORAL LOBE (CEREBRUM)

CEREBELLUM

MEDULLA OBLONGATA (BRAIN STEM)

CATTITUDE

If cats are so smart, why aren't there seeing-eye cats and police cats? Experts think it comes down to attitude—cats just can't be bothered! Dogs, which are naturally social, have been domesticated over thousands of years to please humans. Cats, on the other hand, have evolved to enjoy our company—but they're not hardwired to do our bidding. Maybe they're too smart for that!

EARS WIDE
AT THE BASE

Though very popular in their native country, Australian mists are **NOT OFTEN SEEN OUTSIDE THE LAND DOWN UNDER.**

SLEEK
TABBY
COAT

BROAD
CHEST

PALE
UNDER-
PARTS

AUSTRALIAN MIST

Australia's only pedigreed breed of cat, the Australian mist looks more like a tiny jungle creature than a gentle pet. A breeder named Truda Straede thought that her home of Australia needed its own kind of cat, so she set out to create one.

Over multiple generations, she crossed Burmese (p. 58) for their colors and laid-back personalities, Abyssinians (p. 28) for their coat ticking and intelligence, and Australian domestic shorthair cats (the Australian moggy) for their good health. Nine years later, in 1977, the Australian mist became an official breed.

Australian mists are medium-size cats with large eyes and ears. They have a short coat and a long, thick tail. They come in a range of spotted and marbled patterns and colors, but what makes them special is the ticking from their Abyssinian ancestors, which gives their coats a "misted" effect. It can take until the cats are two years old for their coat colors to fully develop. Their short coats don't require much grooming—though they like the attention anyway!

Australian mists are popular pets because of their easygoing personalities. They don't mind being handled, so they're good choices for families with young children. Australian mists love their humans and want to be around them at all times. That makes them great cats for elderly people or people who work at home. They don't often beg to go outside, preferring to stay indoors with their family.

CAT STATS

FROM: Australia

SIZE: 8-13 pounds (3.5-6 kg)

COAT: Spotted or marbled tabby with ticking; can be brown, peach, chocolate, lilac, and gold

GROOMING:

CATTITUDE: Loving and faithful

"NECKLACE" MARKINGS

BENGAL

With their spotted coats and large size, Bengals look like they would be more at home in the wild than on the couch. That's because one of their ancestors really was a wild animal: an Asian leopard cat, which lives in India, China, and Southeast Asia.

In the 1970s, a scientist named Willard Centerwall at Loyola Marymount University in California, U.S.A., became interested in creating a breed of cat immune to feline leukemia, a disease that has a preventative vaccine but no cure. Because Asian leopard cats are naturally resistant to the disease, Centerwall thought that if he crossed them with domestic cats, the leopards might pass on their immunity. His idea didn't work, but the striking kittens born from the project caught the attention of cat breeders. They crossed the half-leopard kittens with Abyssinians (p. 28), British shorthairs (p. 50), and Egyptian maus (p. 74). Many generations later, they had created a cat they called the leopardette, now named the Bengal.

Bengals are famous for their coats: Their fur is short, thick, and luxurious. Some Bengals' coats have a glittering sheen that makes them look like each hair is dipped in gold. Like their jungle ancestors, Bengals are spotted—even on their bellies. They have strong, muscular bodies and can weigh as much as 22 pounds (10 kg).

Bengals have a lot of energy. They're not gentle lap cats; they like to play games, learn tricks, climb to high places—and even turn light switches on and off! If they get bored, they can be destructive, so Bengals need lots of toys and playtime, and they love an outdoor enclosure where they can climb and bird watch.

CAT STATS

FROM: United States

SIZE: 12–22 pounds (5.5–10 kg)

COAT: Brown, blue, silver, and snow colors in tabby patterns

GROOMING:

CATTITUDE: Friendly and active

Petting a Bengal can feel **LIKE PETTING A SOFT, SILKY RABBIT!**

LONG BODY

LUXURIOUS COAT

THICK TAIL

STRONG LEGS

LARGE PAWS

Bengals love water.

These funny felines like to play in the sink and can often be found lurking nearby when you're brushing your teeth. Some even like to join you in the shower or take a swim with you in the pool! Bengals are great at fishing, so their owners need to make sure to keep their cats' curious paws away from aquariums.

Bengals are social cats that love to hang out with anybody: children, visitors, and cat-friendly dogs. Like the wild animals they resemble, Bengal cats have strong hunting instincts and need to be kept away from small animals like hamsters and guinea pigs. These friendly cats love attention and always want to be near people—many Bengals even love to sleep in their owners' bed with them.

Bengal cats are one of the newest cat breeds, and they weren't fully recognized until 1991. They became popular so quickly that a British woman once paid more than $50,000 for her Bengal. She called the breed the "Rolls-Royce" of cats!

SLEEK
BLACK COAT

This cat has black fur, but that's not all. Its **SKIN AND EVEN THE PADS OF ITS PAWS ARE BLACK.**

ROUNDED HEAD

ROUNDED PAWS

BOMBAY

You might think this cat looks like a pint-size black panther—and that's exactly what breeders of the Bombay had in mind when they set out to create this playful kitty with the glossy black coat.

The Bombay is named for an old city in India where wild, full-size black panthers live. But this miniature version is native to the United States. Breeders crossed Burmese (p. 58) cats with coats in a dark brown color called sable with black American shorthairs (p. 34) to create the new breed. The Bombay was officially recognized in 1978.

Like the wild cat that inspired it, the Bombay is a muscular feline with piercing copper-colored eyes and a sleek and shiny jet-black coat. Unlike a black panther, however, the Bombay is a gentle, loving pet. Like its Burmese relatives, Bombays are playful creatures who would rather chase a toy or hide in a box than snooze on the sofa. Some would call these cats mischievous, but Bombay owners say their cats' antics mostly just make them laugh—kind of like a cross between a dog, a cat, and a monkey!

Bombays are never too far from the humans they adore. Sometimes called "Velcro cats," they are extremely affectionate animals known to follow their humans from room to room and even sleep under the covers. Many Bombay owners have taught their kitties to walk on a leash. The sight of a petite panther out for a walk is sure to turn some heads!

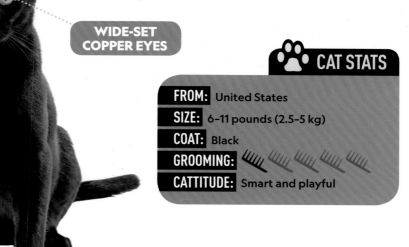

WIDE-SET COPPER EYES

CAT STATS

FROM: United States
SIZE: 6–11 pounds (2.5–5 kg)
COAT: Black
GROOMING:
CATTITUDE: Smart and playful

BRITISH
SHORTHAIR

In Lewis Carroll's famous story *Alice's Adventures in Wonderland*, Alice meets a talking cat with a big grin. This character, the Cheshire Cat, was inspired by a real-life breed: the British shorthair, known as the "smiling cat." These felines aren't very common in the United States, but in the United Kingdom, they are the most popular cat of all.

British shorthairs are one of the oldest known pedigreed cat breeds. Experts think they may even be descended from the cats the ancient Romans kept 2,000 years ago. Cat shows became popular in England during the Victorian era, in the late 19th century, and British shorthairs were the only official breed on display. Today, all cat associations recognize the breed.

British shorthairs are descended from cats who worked for a living, keeping farms and homes pest free. They have sturdy, powerful bodies and large heads with full cheeks. Because of their round faces and velvety coats, they're sometimes called the "teddy bear cat." They come in all colors, from solid black to orange tabby to tortie. But the most popular color is a rich blue-gray. That's why years ago this cat was called the British blue.

British shorthairs are known for their natural smiles. Today, most of these friendly felines are pets who would rather laze by a warm fire than stalk mice in a drafty barn. British shorthairs are regal and calm, and they don't make too much noise or demand attention. Most don't like to be picked up, but they follow their owners from room to room. They're always up for a cuddle, and their plushy coats make them nice for snuggling. Even though they like people, British shorthairs are okay with having alone time, too. That makes them a good choice for people who are busy at work or school during the day.

CAT STATS

FROM: United Kingdom
SIZE: 9–18 pounds (4–8 kg)
COAT: Nearly all colors and patterns
GROOMING:
CATTITUDE: Sweet and affectionate

SMALL
EARS

LARGE
HEAD

FULL
CHEEKS

SLIGHTLY
TAPERING
TAIL

POWERFUL
BODY

These felines **PREFER TO SIT QUIETLY** near their owners, observing what's going on.

If you want a companion with lots of energy, British shorthairs might not be the best choice for you. They're not the type to run around the house, leaping off the furniture; British shorthairs prefer to keep all four paws on the ground. That might be because they're not very athletic: These cats are known for their clumsiness, and they're far too dignified to show it!

When visitors come over, British shorthairs can be a little shy, but they warm up quickly. They sport a mellow temperament and make great family companions. Friendly with children, they can get along with all kinds of pets, from dogs to other cats and even to—with a proper introduction—rabbits and birds. It's no wonder they're the most popular cat in the United Kingdom!

PLAY TIME!

Tearing through the house, hiding inside a paper bag left on the floor, or pouncing—it may seem like it's all just for fun, but playtime has a purpose. Cats use it to practice the moves they need to find, stalk, and catch prey. Starting as young kittens, wild felines play to survive. Domestic cats might not need to hunt for their dinner, but they haven't lost the instinct to frisk and frolic.

HIDING

Humans might see a cardboard box on the floor as recycling waiting to happen—but a cat has a very different idea. As all cat owners know, most cats will immediately adopt a leftover box, grocery bag, or suitcase as a favorite new hidey-hole.

Cats seek out enclosed spaces because they instinctively like to hide. From inside the confines of a hole in a tree—or a basket full of clean laundry—a cat feels safe and secure. They can watch for prey without worrying about predators. And if a bird or rodent wanders by, the cat can dash out from its hiding spot and pounce. But their love of hiding sometimes gets cats in trouble; they've been known to settle for a snooze in the washing machine and even get trapped in the walls of houses under construction!

CLIMBING

If you can't find your cat, chances are you just need to look up: Whether they're napping or just relaxing, cats like to do it from an elevated location. That might be the top of the refrigerator or the highest shelf in a closet. You might never be able to figure out how she gets up there, but you know your kitty loves to have a good view.

Cats like to climb because it gives them a high vantage point from which to spot their prey: animals like mice and birds. But cats are prey themselves to bigger animals, like hawks, owls, and coyotes. Staying up high also helps cats spot—and stay safe from—these hunters. Sleeping in a tree might not sound very fun for a person, but it's how wild cats survive!

STALKING

With her belly nearly touching the ground, the cat moves slowly and stealthily, paws not making a sound. Every muscle is tensed, and her eyes and ears are laser-focused on her "prey"—a dust bunny on the floor.

In the wild, cats stalk to survive. But stalking only works at a distance because cats have a blind spot under their noses. Once a cat gets close to its prey, its eyes aren't useful anymore—so its whiskers take over instead.

Remember that whiskers are a powerful sensory tool that detect changes in air currents; they send signals to the cat's brain telling it exactly where the prey is located. Then, snap!—the cat nabs its dinner. Scientists have timed this event, from the moment a cat's whiskers touched a mouse to the moment the cat pounced, at one-tenth of a second—faster than the blink of an eye!

POUNCING

When a cat spots prey—or that sneaky dust bunny—in the right spot for attack, she goes into pounce mode. Her eyes wide and ears pointed forward, she crouches down and wiggles her hindquarters. This wiggle move might be adorable, but it's not just for show. She's actually pressing her paws into the ground to help her balance her body for the perfect pounce. Cats have to aim their pounces perfectly, because if they miss, they can't just take a second pounce. They're hardwired to start their hunting sequence all over again: spotting, stalking, and then finally pouncing.

CHASING

Your cat might stalk a piece of stray dryer lint, pounce on it, and hold it between her front paws, kicking it with her back legs. She's practicing the same behavior that she would use to catch and kill prey in the wild. Cats are happiest when they get lots of stalking, chasing, and pouncing practice. They like toys that move, make noise, or have an interesting texture. Store-bought toys like play wands and battery-operated toys are good choices. But your kitty will like something you can make at home—like a paper ball or a piece of string tied to a ruler—just as much!

HOW DO CATS ALWAYS LAND
ON THEIR FEET?

A cat is up in a tree, stalking a bird. The bird hops out to the end of a thin branch and, unaware of what's about to happen, opens its beak to sing. The cat moves soundlessly toward its prey, its footfalls nearly silent. It reaches out for the bird when—SNAP!—the branch breaks. The cat goes tumbling downward. But as it falls, its body twists to bring its legs underneath it. The cat lands safely on its feet and scampers away, its pride the only thing injured. What's the secret behind this trick?

CAT TRICK

Cats' ability to seemingly always land on their feet—called the righting reflex—has baffled scientists for more than a century. To turn its body so its feet are the first thing that hits the ground, the cat needs to push against something—but there's nothing to push against in midair. So what's its secret?

STUNT SAFETY

It's true that cats have an uncanny ability to land safely. But don't be tempted to conduct your own cat-falling experiments: The righting reflex isn't fail-safe, and cats still end up in veterinarians' offices with broken legs from falls they couldn't recover from. Keep your cat safe by installing screens in upper windows.

AMAZING ACROBATICS

The mystery remained until 2016, when scientists filmed an African caracal (a type of wild cat) falling. By analyzing the video in slow-motion, they were able to figure out what the cat's body was doing as it went from wild fall to controlled landing.

The scientists observed that when it starts to fall, the caracal's flexible spine immediately goes into action. It rotates the front of its body—its head and front legs—one direction, while spinning the back half—its hind legs and tail—the opposite way. By spinning in two different directions at the same time, the caracal pushes against itself.

While it does this, the cat pulls its front paws close, like a spinning dancer pulling her arms close. That makes the front half of its body spin toward the ground faster than the back half. As its front paws center over the ground, the cat uses the twist in its spine to whip its back legs around. Midair acrobatics accomplished, the cat lands on its feet. What a feline feat!

GOLD OR
YELLOW EYES

MUSCULAR BODY

SHORT,
SATINY
COAT

BURMESE

Burmese are sometimes called "bricks wrapped in silk" because they're heavy for their size and have a soft coat. The breed first came about in 1930, when a man named Dr. Joseph Thompson brought a small brown cat home to the United States with him after a trip to Myanmar (a country formerly called Burma).

Dr. Thompson named the new member of his family Wong Mau and crossed her with Siamese cats (p. 138). The kittens had a unique solid brown coat called sable—the first recognized color of the breed. Today, Burmese are found in warm beige, gray, and many other colors in addition to the original sable color.

These cats have large, round eyes and silky coats that beg to be petted. Burmese grow very attached to their owners and like to be with them as much as possible. As kittens, these cats are very playful, and they keep that energy well into adulthood. Burmese love to play games and enjoy having toys around—though many are also happy to explore the world from a high shelf or their owner's shoulder.

A Burmese may not be the best choice for an owner who spends a lot of time away from home—or one that doesn't care for a feline companion when he or she is reading a book, working at the computer, or watching TV!

Burmese thrive on **LOTS OF HUMAN ATTENTION.**

EARS ROUND AT TIPS

DAINTY LEGS AND PAWS

CAT STATS

FROM: Burma, now called Myanmar

SIZE: 8-14 pounds (3.5-6.5 kg)

COAT: Solid and tortie colors, including blue, brown, cream, lilac, and red, in sepia pattern

GROOMING:

CATTITUDE: Sweet and affectionate

BURMILLA

The Burmilla was created by accident, when a Burmese (p. 58) belonging to an English baroness escaped and mated with a Persian chinchilla (p. 220). Both cats are known for their beautiful coats, and so it's no surprise that their offspring were born with exceptionally attractive fur.

Burmillas also have distinctive markings—their lips, nose, and eyes are all outlined in dark fur. That makes this cat extra expressive, adding to its charm. But they're best known for their dense, silky coats: Their hairs have a silver or gold background color, and they're tipped or shaded in a contrasting color, like brown, blue, or lilac.

Like their Burmese relatives, Burmillas remain playful into adulthood. Unlike most cats, they're known to be klutzes, so they might not be the best choice for owners with a taste for expensive breakables. Though they are affectionate, they don't demand as much attention as a Burmese: They'll curl up in your lap only if invited.

Burmillas are generally gentle cats that make good pets for families. They get along well with children and cat-friendly dogs. Though it isn't very well-known, this unique breed is growing in popularity as more people discover its charms.

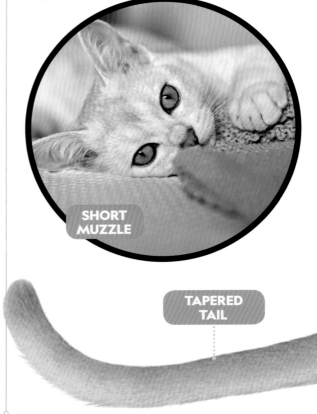

SHORT MUZZLE

TAPERED TAIL

🐾 CAT STATS

FROM: United Kingdom

SIZE: 9–15 pounds (4–7 kg)

COAT: Shaded colors including lilac, black, brown, blue, and tortie

GROOMING:

CATTITUDE: Loving and affectionate

Most Burmillas are short-haired, but **OCCASIONALLY, A LONG-HAIRED KITTEN IS BORN** to short-haired parents.

ROUND FACE

DENSE COAT

COMPACT BODY

A Chartreux is the official mascot of the annual **MONTREUX JAZZ FESTIVAL** in Montreux, Switzerland.

FULL CHEEKS

SOLID BODY

ROUND HEAD

BLUE LIPS

CHARTREUX

There are many legends about the origins of the elegant blue cats known as Chartreux. Some say they first lived with the Carthusian Order of monks in France. These quiet and dignified cats would have made great companions for the monks—and kept the rodent population in the monastery under control.

The only thing known about the Chartreux' history is that it is one of the oldest cat breeds there is. This gentle feline is also an unofficial national symbol of its home country, France. French president Charles de Gaulle, who served from 1959 to 1969, famously owned a Chartreux named Gris-Gris. Stories say that the statesman's feline friend was never far from his side and liked to follow the president from room to room.

It wasn't until after World War I that French cat fanciers began to breed this cat. They gathered up as many as they could find, created a breed standard, and began showing their cats in Europe in the 1920s or 1930s. These cats are still uncommon outside of their home country, but they're becoming more widely known. The breed was recognized by the Cat Fanciers' Association in 1987.

Chartreux are known to be extremely intelligent cats. Owners tell stories of Chartreux who have learned how to work buttons, play with alarm clocks, and open latches. Though they're smart, these cats are very quiet. When they do meow, most Chartreux have a soft voice. They have a personality to match—undemanding and gentle. Chartreux love attention and become devoted to people who give them tickles under the chin and rubs between the ears. They like to snuggle and can often be found on their owners' beds. Once a Chartreux has bonded to you, you truly have a friend for life.

COAT IS SLIGHTLY WOOLLY TO THE TOUCH

CAT STATS

FROM: France
SIZE: 7–17 pounds (3–7.5 kg)
COAT: Blue-gray only
GROOMING:
CATTITUDE: Quiet and affectionate

AMAZING TONGUES

If your dog doesn't get a bath for a few weeks, he probably gets pretty stinky. But many cats go their whole lives *never* having a good scrub. Instead, cats bathe by cleaning themselves with their tongues. What's their secret to keeping clean without soap and water? One scientist decided to find out—and she was surprised by what she discovered.

UP-CLOSE LOOK

Alexis Noel was home for the holidays, relaxing in front of the TV with the family cats, when one of them decided to lick a blanket on the couch—and got his tongue stuck to it! He got loose before long, but it made Noel—a mechanical engineer at the Georgia Institute of Technology in Atlanta—curious about the sticky scenario. Back at the lab, she and her team used high-speed video cameras to record a cat licking up food wedged into a fur mat.

The scientists already knew that cats' tongues are covered in teeny spines called filiform papillae. These are what gives their tongues their rough, sandpaper-like texture. By watching their slow-motion video, the researchers discovered that these spines are sharp and curved—kind of like a cat's claws. The spines glide through fur but catch when they hit a tangle. Then, the spines rotate, digging into the knot and pulling it apart. The spines also grab dirt and food particles stuck in the fur.

CAT POWERED

Noel and her team think cats' tongues have the potential to do more than keep Fluffy clean: They could someday inspire new technology, such as parts for robots. Conventional robots are made of hard parts, which aren't good at tasks like gripping delicate items. A material modeled after cat tongues could give a robot's grasping arm a more sensitive grip, allowing them to grab something like a delicate glass without breaking it.

Noel thinks the research could also lead to improvements in an everyday item: the ordinary hairbrush. A hairbrush designed after a cat's tongue could be easier to clean and better at combing through tangles without pain. Who knew your kitty's tongue was so high-tech?

CHAUSIE

Every house kitty has a little bit of jungle cat inside it. But the chausie (pronounced chow-see) is especially wild. That's because this unusual breed came about in the 1960s, when jungle cats, a wild species of cat (*Felis chaus*) found in the swamps of South and Central Asia, were crossed with domestic shorthairs, creating a hybrid.

With their large ears and big, muscular bodies with extra-long legs, chausies look a little bit like miniature cougars. Their exotic looks are topped off with their coats, which come in striking shades of black and ticked tabby.

This is not your average family cat, and experts recommend that only experienced cat owners who have plenty of time to devote to their pets take them on. With their athletic abilities and wild nature, chausies can be destructive when bored, quickly learning how to open cupboards and wreak havoc. Children shouldn't be around this breed without close supervision.

For the right cat owner, though, chausies can be lots of fun. With their sporty physique, these cats can leap more than six feet (2 m) in the air! They love chasing toys and are always up for a play session with their owners.

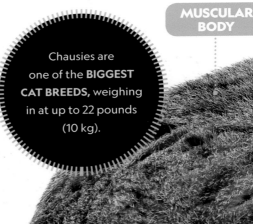

MUSCULAR BODY

Chausies are one of the **BIGGEST CAT BREEDS,** weighing in at up to 22 pounds (10 kg).

🐾 CAT STATS

FROM: United States

SIZE: 12–22 pounds (5.5–10 kg)

COAT: Black solid and ticked tabby in brown and black

GROOMING:

CATTITUDE: Intelligent and energetic

LARGE,
TUFTED
EARS

EXTRA-
LONG LEGS

HAIRLESS OUTER EAR

LARGE, OVAL EYES

HIGH CHEEKBONES

WAVY COAT

These cats
**SOMETIMES HAVE
TO HAVE BATHS—**
like dogs.

CORNISH REX

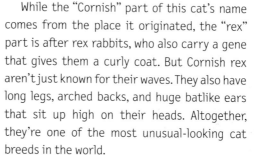

In 1950, a farm cat in Cornwall, England, gave birth to a litter of kittens. Four of them looked alike, but one stood out for his odd, curly coat. The cat's owners were infatuated with the unusual kitten. They named him Kallibunker and began trying to find a way to create more curly-coated kittens.

There are lots of stories about how Kallibunker got his wavy fur. One far-out theory says that it was the result of a high dose of radiation from nearby tin mines! But the truth is that Kallibunker's curly coat was the result of a natural genetic mutation. Kallibunker's offspring were crossed with other breeds, such as American shorthairs (p. 34), British shorthairs (p. 50), and Siamese (p. 138) until the modern Cornish rex was created.

While the "Cornish" part of this cat's name comes from the place it originated, the "rex" part is after rex rabbits, who also carry a gene that gives them a curly coat. But Cornish rex aren't just known for their waves. They also have long legs, arched backs, and huge batlike ears that sit up high on their heads. Altogether, they're one of the most unusual-looking cat breeds in the world.

Cornish rexes' curly coats lack an outer layer to absorb oils from their skin, so their owners must bathe their cats occasionally to keep them clean. Many Cornish rexes don't mind too much—these cats are extremely social and affectionate, and many can be taught to perform tricks. These curly cats make devoted pets who follow their owners around and want nothing more than a cuddle—and maybe a game of chase.

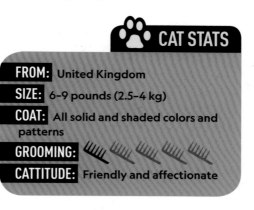

LONG, SLENDER TAIL

SLENDER LEGS

CAT STATS

FROM: United Kingdom

SIZE: 6–9 pounds (2.5–4 kg)

COAT: All solid and shaded colors and patterns

GROOMING: 🖌🖌🖌🖌🖌

CATTITUDE: Friendly and affectionate

DEVON REX

"The poodle cat" and "the alien" cat are nicknames for this striking feline—but its real name is the Devon rex.

Like the Cornish rex (p. 68), the "rex" part of the Devon rex's name comes from curly-coated rex rabbits. But even though it looks like it could be the Cornish rex's cousin, the Devon rex gets its curls from a different genetic mutation. That means the Devon rex is a unique breed.

Devon rex have fine, short, wavy coats that—unlike most cats' coats—have no long "guard hairs." That means there isn't a lot of fur between the Devon rex's skin and the outside air, so these kitties can get chilly. Some owners even put them in sweaters when the weather gets cold. Each cat's coat is unique, with a different amount of wave and curl.

Devons love to be the center of attention. They like to get right in the action by perching on their favorite person's shoulder and even take part in the conversation with soft meows. Devons are friendly with their family, visitors, and children. They love to learn tricks, and many Devon owners have taught their feline friends to play fetch. At night, these cuddly cats can be found snoozing with their owners, and—because they get cold easily—many sleep under the covers.

Devon rex's enormous ears look like **SATELLITE DISHES.**

🐾 CAT STATS

FROM: United Kingdom
SIZE: 6–9 pounds (2.5–4 kg)
COAT: All colors, shades, and patterns
GROOMING:
CATTITUDE: Social and cuddly

LARGE EARS

SMALL
HEAD AND
LONG NECK

CURLY COAT

MUSCULAR
BODY

VERY LARGE EARS

SLANTING GREEN EYES

The Donskoy's **SKIN IS SOFT AND WARM** to the touch.

STRONG BODY

DONSKOY

In 1987, a frightened kitten was rescued from the streets of Rostov-on-Don in the Soviet Union—now called Russia. When the kitten grew up, its hair fell out. The kitten's owner tried in vain to find a cure for her little friend's baldness, but the fur never grew back. When the kitten became a cat and had kittens of her own, some were completely hairless. Others had fur that fell out, just like their mother's had.

The Donskoy, also called the Don sphynx, is not a cat for everyone. Some people find its bald skin and wrinkled face endearing. Others think this cat is downright frightening. Slanting green eyes, a whiplike tail, and extra-long toes only add to this cat's strange appearance. Whether they like the Donskoy or not, everyone agrees that this breed turns heads.

Many Donskoy are truly bald, but some have a partial coat that can be velvety or wavy in texture. But just because they're considered hairless doesn't mean they don't need grooming. Donskoys must be bathed regularly to remove oils from their skin. Because its skin is exposed, the Donskoy needs protection from the sun in the summer and extra layers to keep warm in the winter.

Not everybody loves the Donskoy at first sight. But their owners say this cat is extremely friendly, gentle, and good-natured. They're social creatures who will make friends with the family dog and get lonely if they are left alone often. That makes these odd cats not only eye-catching but good pets, too.

FOLDS ON FOREHEAD

EXTRA-LONG, WEBBED TOES

CAT STATS

FROM: Russia

SIZE: 8–15 pounds (3.5–7 kg)

COAT: All colors, shades, and patterns

GROOMING:

CATTITUDE: Social and loving

LONG, THIN TAIL

EGYPTIAN MAU

Egyptian maus make great pets—even the ancient Egyptians thought so. "Mau" is the Egyptian word for cat. Some experts think that the spotted, long-bodied cats painted on ancient Egyptian tombs and temples may be the distant ancestors of the modern mau. If that's true, the ancient Egyptians loved the mau's ancestors so much that they had their kitties mummified to keep them company in the afterlife.

The modern Egyptian mau traces its origins back only about half a century, to a silver kitten that was a given as a gift to a Russian princess. The princess named the kitten Baba and brought the cat and two of her kittens along when she moved to the United States in 1956. There, she began officially breeding Egyptian maus to make sure the breed would survive after she was gone.

With its spotted coat in silver, bronze, or smoke, and large green eyes, maus are striking felines. And that spotted coat occurred naturally, not as a result of selective breeding by humans—that makes the mau the only naturally spotted domesticated cat in the world.

Maus are strong, athletic cats that love to show off their hunting and stalking skills with toys. They are devoted pets that love their families and express their happiness with little chirping noises called chortles. Maus love to jump and climb, and many even like to play in water, so don't be surprised to find your mau with his paw in the sink!

CAT STATS

FROM: Egypt

SIZE: 6–11 pounds (2.5–5 kg)

COAT: Spotted silver and bronze, black smoke with tabby markings

GROOMING:

CATTITUDE: Active and devoted

HIND LEGS LONGER THAN FRONT LEGS

SPOTTED COAT

ALMOND-SHAPED EYES

The Egyptian mau **LOOKS LIKE A LITTLE CHEETAH**—and acts like one, too.

CATS IN ANCIENT EGYPT

Pets were popular in ancient Egypt. Some were exotic—like baboons, hippos, and even lions! But, just like modern animal lovers, ancient Egyptians loved to keep a cat or two around, too. These animals were more than pets, though: Their humans worshipped them as gods.

Welcome to the TEMPLE OF BASTET

The ancient Egyptians thought many animals were sacred; for example, they valued dogs for their ability to hunt and protect the family. But cats were given special status. The Egyptians believed felines were magical creatures who could bring good luck to those they lived with.

Around 1500 B.C., there was a religious group devoted to worshipping a cat goddess named Bastet, the goddess of music and joy, and protector of women. Bastet was originally pictured as a lion, but later, statues and other art showed her as a woman with the head of a cat, sometimes surrounded by a group of kittens. Bastet was so popular that she had a temple built in her honor in the city of Per-Bast, where Egyptians traveled from all over to worship.

Though they were most sacred in ancient Egypt, cats did appear in the myths and religions of many other cultures. The Norse goddess Freya drove a chariot pulled not by horses but by two giant gray cats. The Hindu goddess Shashthi was often depicted riding a cat (pictured). And Islamic texts taught that the "M" mark on many a tabby cat's forehead was put there by the Prophet Muhammad's touch.

GODDESSES ON EARTH

The Egyptians thought of cats as earthly representations of the goddess Bastet. They honored them in carvings (top photo, above), paintings, and sculptures. They treated their cats as treasured pets, dressing them in jewels and feeding them special treats. They considered killing a cat a serious crime, and those who did—even by accident—were sentenced to death.

When a cat died, its owners went into mourning. They shaved off their eyebrows and remained in a period of grief until their eyebrows grew back. If they were wealthy enough, they would even have their beloved pet mummified (bottom photo, above) and buried in a decorative sarcophagus. Priests presented these animals to the gods to show the dedication of their owners. No other culture in history has revered cats as highly as the ancient Egyptians.

CAT SUPERSTITIONS

Felines were long believed to be supernatural creatures that associated with evil spirits. With their all-seeing eyes and silent way of moving, cats *do* seem to have a little something magical about them. Cultures from all over the world have myths and superstitions about the cats that walk among us. But are they nothing more than tall tales?

WITCHCRAFT AT WORK

Centuries ago, people thought witches weren't just for Halloween—they were real-life creatures who came over from the dark side to cast spells on unlucky humans. In the Middle Ages, people believed that every witch had a "familiar"—a demon sidekick that took the form of an animal. That led to many little old ladies who kept cuddly cats being accused of witchcraft. Other people thought that cats were actually witches themselves; they believed these wicked women could shape-shift, and so a stray cat on the street could really be an evil witch in disguise.

BLACK LUCK

In the United States and some parts of Europe, it's believed that black cats are unlucky. As the superstition goes, if one of these creatures crosses your path, you're doomed. But in Britain, the opposite is true: In fact, if a new bride and groom come across a black cat on their wedding day, it's said that they're guaranteed a long and happy marriage.

LUCKY CHARMS

In some cultures, cats are considered good luck. In Russia, new parents used to put a cat in the baby's cradle to keep away evil spirits. (Of course, it's never a good idea to use a pet as a babysitter unsupervised.) Silkworm farmers in China also thought cats could keep away bad vibes: They used cats—or pictures of them—to guard their cocoons from the mice that preyed on the silkworms. And rice farmers would carry a cat around in a basket for families to sprinkle with water, a practice they believed would bring rain to their crops.

SHIP'S MATE

Some feline folktales say that cats have mysterious power over the weather. Some stories claim they can bring a storm by clawing at the furniture; others say if a cat sneezes it means rain is coming. These tales may have begun with sailors, who not only had a reputation for being extra-superstitious but also were constantly concerned about the weather. Some ships would include a cat in their crew for good luck (and rodent control)—but the sailors were careful never to speak the feline's name, as that was considered a guarantee of bad luck.

NINE LIVES

The idea that cats have nine lives is a long-lived myth itself. It can be traced back as far as 1595, when playwright William Shakespeare referenced it in *Romeo and Juliet*. The myth probably came about because cats—with their quick reflexes and ability to seemingly always land on their feet—do seem remarkably good at getting themselves out of sticky situations.

FELINE FOLKTALES

Cats have starred in folktales for thousands of years. In ancient times, they were often cast as mythical beasts that flew alongside dragons and unicorns. During the Middle Ages, cats got a reputation for being unlucky, and after that, they appeared as clever helpers in some tales and as sneaky villains in others. Here are two folktales starring these whiskered characters.

WHY DOG AND CAT ARE ENEMIES
Adapted from a Chinese folktale

Today, it is often said that dogs and cats don't get along. But once upon a time, they were the best of friends. Back then, there was a man and his wife who had a dog and a cat as pets. They had a lucky life, with a nice place to call home and plenty of food to eat. They didn't know it, but the cause of their good fortune was a gold ring they possessed.

One day, not knowing the ring was magic, the man and his wife sold it. No sooner was the deed done than they fell on hard times. Soon, they no longer had a nice place to call home or enough food to eat. As the man and his wife suffered, the cat and dog grew worried.

"We must get the magic ring back for them," said the dog.

"You are right," said the cat. "But how do we do that? The ring has been locked away in a chest by its new owner."

The dog and cat thought and thought. Finally, they came up with a plan. "I will catch a mouse," said the cat. "Then, I will have the mouse gnaw a hole in the chest where the ring is kept so we can fetch the ring."

So the cat went out and caught a mouse, and she began to carry it to the house where the ring was kept. But on the way, she came upon a wide river. She could not cross it herself. So the dog had the cat climb on his back, and he carried her and the mouse across the river. The cat brought the mouse into the house, where it gnawed a hole in the chest, and the cat carried out the ring. Holding the ring in her mouth, she went back to the river, and the dog carried her across once more.

Full of excitement, the two animals raced home. The cat hopped from rooftop to rooftop, while the dog had to run along the ground and go around the houses. So the cat got home first.

"What a good and smart creature the cat is!" said the man and his wife when they saw the cat with the magic ring. "She is clearly the better of our two animals—for where is the dog?" And they praised and petted the cat and let her sit by the fire.

When the dog came home panting a while later, the cat sat purring by the fire. She didn't say a word about how the dog had helped get the magic ring back. Angry, the dog chased after her, snapping and barking. And ever since that day, the dog and cat have been enemies.

PUSS IN BOOTS
Adapted from a European folktale

Once upon a time, there was a poor miller. All he had to pass on to his three sons was his mill, his donkey, and his cat. The eldest son took the mill. The middle son took the donkey. And for the youngest, there was nothing left but the cat.

The youngest son despaired. How could he make a living from a meager little cat? So the cat comforted him, saying, "Don't worry, master. If you will just give me a bag and a pair of boots, so that I may tromp off through the world, then you'll see that you didn't get such a bad deal."

So the miller's son did what the cat asked. The cat put his paws in his shiny new boots, slung his bag over his shoulder, and was off into the world. He first went to a field, where he put some greens into his bag, left the bag in a meadow, and waited for a rabbit to come along. Sure enough, a wiggly-nosed rabbit hopped over and, smelling the greens, jumped right into the bag.

The cat picked up the bag with the rabbit inside and went to the palace, where he asked to speak with the king. He said, "Your Majesty, please accept this gift from my master, the Marquis of Carabas."

That wasn't the miller's son's name, of course, but the king didn't know that. "Tell your master he has my thanks, and I am very pleased with his gift," said the king.

Then, the cat scampered home. He waited for a day when he knew the king was to be out driving with his beautiful daughter, the princess. And on that day, the cat said to his master, "If you hear me now and follow my advice, your fortune will be made. All you have to go do is jump in the river alongside the road."

The miller's son was confused by the cat's strange instructions, but he followed them nonetheless. While he was in the water, the king and his daughter passed by the river. The cat shouted, "Help! Help! The Marquis of Carabas is going to be drowned!"

The king, eager to help, leaped out of his carriage and commanded his guards to pull the miller's son out of the water. Thinking the boy was the Marquis of Carabas, the king brought him to the castle and gave him some of his own fine clothes to replace his sopping wet ones.

When the princess saw the miller's son, all dressed in finery, she fell in love. The king was delighted that his daughter was smitten with someone so fine as the Marquis de Carabas. He threw a wonderful wedding for the pair, and the miller's son lived in riches and finery the rest of his life—all because of the cat's cunning.

SMALL, ROUNDED EARS

BIG, ROUND EYES

FULL FACE

THICK UNDERCOAT

LARGE, ROUNDED PAWS

EXOTIC
SHORTHAIR

With its round body, big eyes, and plushy coat, this breed looks like a stuffed toy. The exotic shorthair's coat is unlike that of any other shorthair cat; soft and thick, it begs to be petted. That's a good thing for this affectionate cat, who loves a cuddle!

Exotic shorthairs came about when breeders wanted the silvery coat and striking green eyes of a Persian (p. 220) in a short-haired package. Starting in the 1950s, they began crossing Persians with American shorthairs, and later, other short-haired breeds such as the Burmese (p. 58) and the Abyssinian (p. 28). The result was a cat with a face and body similar to a Persian's but wrapped in a short-haired coat that is much easier to care for.

For this reason, exotic shorthairs are sometimes called "the lazy man's Persian." They don't need anything more than grooming two or three times a week to keep their coats healthy. Like the Persian, the exotic shorthair has an undercoat of soft hairs that lifts its topcoat away from its body. That's what gives the exotic its plush appearance.

Like their Persian cousins, exotic shorthairs have a round head and short nose. All have somewhat flat faces: Some are so "smushed" that they are prone to breathing problems. They have short legs and sturdy, muscular bodies, but don't mistake this cutie for a tough cat—exotic shorthairs are lovers, not fighters, and they fare best indoors.

SHORT, THICK TAIL

CAT STATS

FROM: United States
SIZE: 8–15 pounds (3.5–7 kg)
COAT: Almost all colors and patterns
GROOMING:
CATTITUDE: Spirited and chatty

Exotic shorthairs come in almost any cat color there is. They can be a solid color, such as white, blue, chocolate, or lilac. They can be shaded silver or golden, tabby, calico, or smoke—or many other colors. Exotic shorthairs have striking eye colors related to their coat colors: Solid-colored exotics have copper eyes, silver and golden ones have green or blue eyes, and white ones have blue or copper eyes—or one eye of each color!

This breed doesn't just look like Persian cats—they act like them, too. Exotics are sweet, docile cats. They're affectionate and are up for a cuddle whenever there's a free lap available. They're known as quiet cats, and when they do speak up, it's in a soft, musical voice. They like company and will follow their owners around, waiting patiently for attention. If they don't get it, they're known to sit in front of their people, staring at them longingly until they're picked up for a hug.

Exotic shorthairs' small, round ears and big, round eyes make them **LOOK LIKE KITTENS EVEN WHEN THEY'RE GROWN UP.**

HAVANA

The Havana cat is a rare breed known for its glossy brown coat in a rich chocolate brown shade. Much about the history of this cat is shrouded in mystery. The Havana can trace its origin back to Southeast Asia, where it was believed to protect its owners from evil. Later, it became known as the Swiss mountain cat, then the Havana brown, and finally the Havana.

The reasons for all those renamings are now lost to history. What is known is that in the 1890s, cat fanciers in Britain began to exhibit brown cats from Thailand that were similar to Siamese. The cats first appeared in the United States in the 1950s. Then, the cat was bred to have two different looks: British breeders crossed it with the Siamese (p. 138), eventually creating the Oriental shorthair (p. 114); American breeders did not, and the result was a cat with a rounder face and shorter body that came to be called the Havana. The breed was officially recognized in 1964.

With its glossy coat and bright green, oval-shaped eyes, the Havana stands out. And if it doesn't get the attention of those around it, this bold and friendly cat will seek it out. Expect your pet Havana to follow you everywhere around the house, always curious about what you're doing.

NARROW HEAD

OVAL FEET

CAT STATS

FROM: United States

SIZE: 9–10 pounds (4–4.5 kg)

COAT: Rich brown and lilac

GROOMING:

CATTITUDE: Affectionate and playful

LARGE
EARS

Havanas are
**PLAYFUL AND
TALKATIVE.**

**RICH
BROWN OR
LILAC COAT**

**STRAIGHT,
SLIM LEGS**

SHORT TAIL ENDS IN A POM-POM OF LONGER HAIRS

SOFT COAT

In Japan, the Japanese bobtail is a **SYMBOL OF GOOD LUCK.**

BROAD MUZZLE

OVAL PAWS

JAPANESE BOBTAIL

If you saw a Japanese bobtail from behind, you might mistake it for a bunny! That's because of the distinctive "pom" tail of the breed that makes it one of the most unusual cats in the world.

Bobtailed cats have lived in Japan for at least 1,000 years. Legend says they first came to the island nation as gifts from the emperor of China to the emperor of Japan. They may have started out as pets for royalty, but they soon became known as excellent pest patrol that could take care of any rodents lurking around grain stores or silkworm farms.

In 1968, three of the cats were imported to the United States, where they became popular for their unique looks and charming personalities. Japanese bobtails are playful, smart cats that love toys or a game of chase. They're active cats that get along well with a friend—their preference is another bobtail, but the family dog will do in a pinch. A companion is a good idea, because if bobtails are bored, these smart felines can sometimes become destructive.

The bobtail has two personality characteristics that make it stand out among cat breeds: They love water and can often be found playing in the sink or—if you're not careful—splashing in the fish tank. And these cats are also extremely talkative. They use a range of soft chirps to let you know what's on their mind at all times.

LARGE, WIDE-SET EARS

🐾 CAT STATS

FROM: Japan
SIZE: 6–9 pounds (2.5–4 kg)
COAT: All colors and patterns
GROOMING:
CATTITUDE: Spirited and chatty

SLEEP SECRETS

Cats sleep a lot—between 16 and 20 hours a day. That's more than most mammals and twice as much as most humans. But why are cats always, well, catnapping?

REST AND RECHARGE

Like a lot of their other behaviors, cats' love of a good snooze harks back to their wild roots. How much wild animals sleep has a lot to do with whether they're predators or prey. Think of animals like gazelles that spend the day grazing the African savanna. That constant energy intake fuels them enough to keep constant watch for their predators—the lions that live on the savanna with them. These big cats can most often be found—you guessed it—zonked out in the shade of a tree.

A cat, whether it's a lion or a domestic shorthair that just *thinks* it's a lion, is evolved to hunt for its dinner. As predators, they have few natural predators of their own, so they don't have to stay awake and vigilant like creatures such as gazelles do. And there's another reason cats love to snooze: Hunting takes a lot of energy. Stalking, pouncing, and wrestling with prey really sap a cat's reserves—so they nap whenever they can, conserving calories for the hunt.

Cats tend to sleep during the day, and they are most active at twilight and dawn—sometimes to the annoyance of their owners, who would rather be relaxing (or snoozing themselves) at these hours.

SLEEP SCIENCE

There are two types of feline sleep: dozing and deep sleep. Dozing cats often lie with their head up and their paws tucked underneath them. Cats can even snooze sitting up, with their muscles tensed to hold them upright. This light sleep allows cats to stay on alert and be ready to spring into action at a moment's notice.

When cats enter deep sleep, their bodies relax. They stretch out and lay on their sides. During this phase, their brain patterns change, becoming similar to their brain patterns when they're awake: This is the phase when cats dream. No one know for sure what kitties dream of, but from the looks of their twitching paws, maybe they spend their dreams hunting.

This deep sleep phase usually lasts for only about five minutes and then switches back to lighter sleep. A cat will alternate between the two sleep phases until it wakes up, yawns, stretches, and stalks off.

DOZING

DEEP SLEEP

KHAO MANEE

Translated from Thai, this cat's name means "white jewel," and this elegant feline has a background to match. It was once considered so special that only Thai royalty could own it. These cats were thought of as sacred: One legend held that their mismatched eyes have mystical powers.

One of Thailand's most famous rulers, King Chulalongkorn—who reigned from 1868 to 1910, when the country was called Siam—bred khao manees. He kept many generations of these cats within the palace walls. It's even said that a khao manee was carried in a ceremonial procession to the throne room when a new king of Siam was crowned in 1926.

Khao manees are always white, though some kittens are born with a dark spot on their heads. Like all white cats, khao manees run the risk of being deaf. That's because the gene that makes an animal's coat white can also affect its hearing.

After its pure white coat, the most striking part of a khao manee is its eyes. They come in many colors, but the most striking is "odd eyes," also called heterochromia, when one is blue and the other is green or gold. Set against their white coats, the khao manee's colorful eyes truly turn heads!

Khao manees were first brought to the United States from Thailand in 1999. In that short time, they've won over a lot of cat lovers. These cats are outgoing and adore the company of people. They're extroverts who boldly greet visitors and thrive on attention from their owners.

CAT STATS

FROM: Thailand
SIZE: 6–12 pounds (2.5–5.5 kg)
COAT: White only
GROOMING:
CATTITUDE: Curious and intelligent

Khao manees are thought to bring **GOOD LUCK** to their humans.

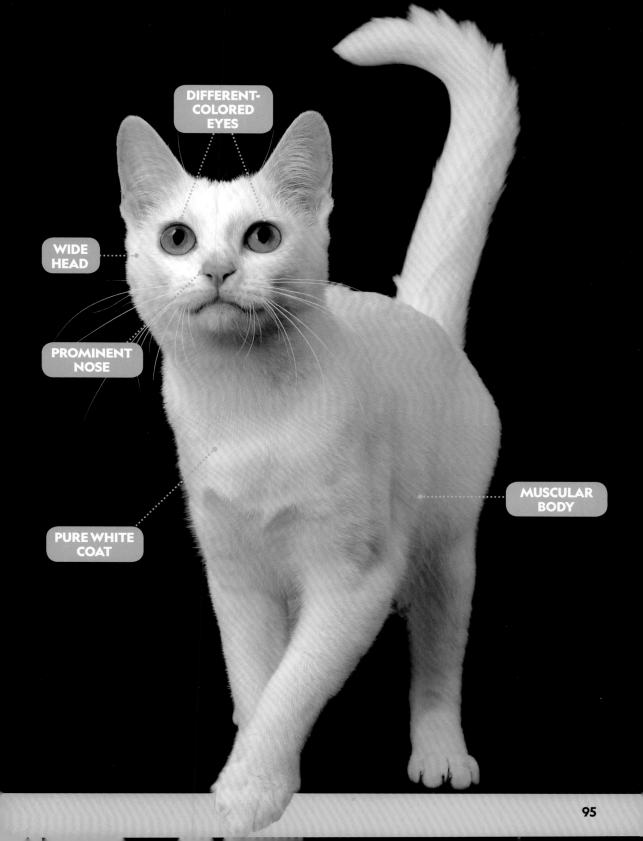

DIFFERENT-COLORED EYES

WIDE HEAD

PROMINENT NOSE

PURE WHITE COAT

MUSCULAR BODY

LARGE, ROUND GREEN EYES

Korats were once prized as **GOOD-LUCK CHARMS.**

SLIM BODY

HEART-SHAPED HEAD

KORAT

There are few breeds more ancient than the Korat. It first appears in a book from Thailand called *The Cat Book Poems* that experts think could date back 800 years. Despite its very old origins, this cat wasn't known in the West until 1959.

In ancient times, Korats were popular gifts—always presented in pairs—and were especially popular as wedding presents, where they were thought to bring prosperity and fortune to the bride and groom in their native country of Thailand. Unlike most breeds, Korats are considered a natural breed that has never been crossed with another kind of cat.

Korats have a beautiful silvery blue coat and large, round, bright green eyes. They have an unusual heart-shaped head and a long, graceful body. Their athletic features aren't just for show: Korats are extremely active cats that love playing, especially with a friend. Perhaps Korats were traditionally given in pairs for a reason; this isn't a cat that likes to be alone. Without enough companionship, these cats can develop behavior problems such as separation anxiety. They consider their people to be the perfect playmates and are known to follow their owners around from room to room.

Korats usually bond with one or two people. They'll spend most of their time with these chosen ones. Aside from their owners, their favorite friend is another Korat, but they've been known to grow attached to the family dog, too.

SILVER-TIPPED HAIRS

BLUE COAT

CAT STATS

FROM: Thailand

SIZE: 6–10 pounds (2.5–4.5 kg)

COAT: Blue only

GROOMING:

CATTITUDE: Graceful and gentle

KURILIAN BOBTAIL

The Kurilian bobtail traces its origins to a remote stretch of islands between Siberia and Japan. There, 56 volcanic islands—the Kuril Islands—stretch for 700 miles (1,127 km) between the Russian peninsula of Kamchatka and the Japanese island Hokkaido. No one knows exactly when these cats came to be, but historical documents show that short-tailed felines have inhabited the islands for at least 200 years.

On the islands where they come from, Kurilians don't just hunt mice and rats: They're also known to catch snakes, hares, squirrels—and even fish. Their excellent hunting abilities made them popular pets, and Kurilians spread to nearby mainland Russia during the 20th century. It is rare to see them outside of Russia, but as more Kurilians are brought to cat shows, the cat world is starting to take notice of this unique breed.

Kurilians have a wild appearance. They almost look like miniature lynx, a type of wild cat. Each Kurilian has a slightly different tail, but all have tails with many kinks that can curl or bend in any direction. Their tails can be made up of as few as two vertebrae—small bones that make up the tail and spine—or as many as 10. Their tails can look like a puffball, or even a spiral. Kurilian owners think their unique tails give these cats a lot of personality.

Kurilian bobtails are gentle cats. They're known for their relaxed personalities, and they get along with other cats, kids, and household pets. They're active cats who love to play, run, and jump. And even though they're great pets, they're still excellent hunters—a bonus for any owners with a pest problem.

CAT STATS

FROM: Kuril Islands, North Pacific
SIZE: 7–10 pounds (3–4.5 kg)
COAT: Most solid colors and shades in bicolor, tortie, and tabby patterns
GROOMING:
CATTITUDE: Gentle and playful

This cat's bobbed tail is the result of a **NATURAL GENETIC MUTATION.**

SHORT, KINKED TAIL

TRIANGULAR EARS

BROAD CHIN

MINIMAL UNDERCOAT

STRONG THIGHS

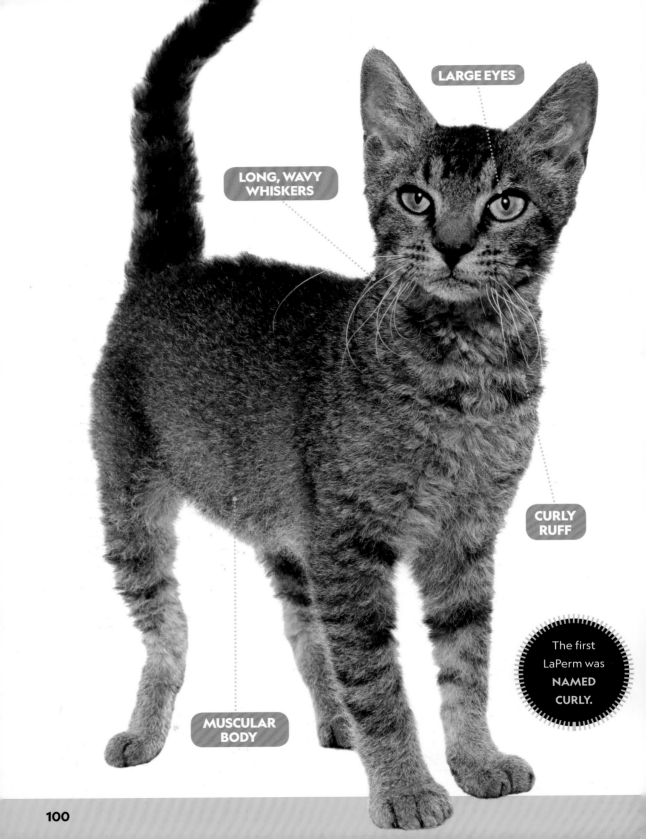

LARGE EYES

LONG, WAVY WHISKERS

CURLY RUFF

MUSCULAR BODY

The first LaPerm was NAMED CURLY.

LAPERM
SHORTHAIR

If you guessed that this cat is named after the "perm," the hair treatment that turns stick-straight locks into curling ringlets, you're right! LaPerms are covered with an unusual curly coat. The long-haired form of this breed (p. 198) can have flowing corkscrew curls, but the LaPerm shorthair's coat often has a "bottle brush" texture, with the hair standing on end away from the coat.

LaPerms first appeared in Oregon, U.S.A., in 1982. One day, a barn cat gave birth to a litter of six kittens. Five looked alike, but one stood out— she was completely bald, with large, wide-spaced ears. A few weeks later, the kitten began growing curly hair. Her owner named the cat Curly. She fell in love with Curly's sweet, trusting personality and soft, wavy coat. Curly gave birth to a number of litters in her lifetime, and many of her kittens inherited her gene for a curling coat.

LaPerm owners love stroking their cats' fur, and their LaPerms love the attention. These cats are gentle and affectionate animals that often purr the moment their owners are near. They're not shy about asking for attention, and they'll rub their noses against yours or lay draped over your shoulder. Even though they are lap cats at heart, LaPerms are a highly active breed. They're curious and always want to know what's going on around them. LaPerms make lively, lovable pets, and their coats make them one of the nicest breeds to cuddle.

CAT STATS

FROM: United States
SIZE: 8–12 pounds (3.5–5.5 kg)
COAT: All colors, shades, and patterns
GROOMING:
CATTITUDE: Sweet and affectionate

TOP 5 MOST FAMOUS
FILM FELINES

From Lassie to Toto, canines usually get top billing when it comes to playing movie pets. While they may not be quite as trainable as dogs, cats can be film stars, too. Check out these five kitty stars of the silver screen.

THE CHESHIRE CAT
from *Alice in Wonderland*

A perfect mix of silly with a dash of sinister, the Cheshire Cat was made famous by Lewis Carroll's book *Alice's Adventures in Wonderland*—but no film fan can forget the pink-and-purple animated version with the big grin. With his manner of talking in circles and his charming-but-eerie smile, he's still one of the story's most recognizable characters, more than 60 years after the movie was made. Fun film fact: The actor who voiced the Cheshire Cat was Sterling Holloway, also the voice of Winnie the Pooh.

CROOKSHANKS
from *Harry Potter*

Scruffy, smart, and a little surly, Crookshanks is Hermione Granger's pet in the *Harry Potter* series. Rescued from Magical Menagerie, the pet shop where he had been for a long time because "nobody wanted him," Crookshanks quickly becomes Hermione's beloved sidekick (even if not everyone likes him). Half-cat, half-catlike magical creature called a Kneazle, Crookshanks has a special ability to spot untrustworthy creatures, which comes in handy during the characters' escapades. He was played by two red Persians, called Crackerjack and Pumpkin, who wore bits of shed fur stuck to their bodies to give them a ragged appearance.

GARFIELD
from *Garfield*

Lazy, sarcastic, and obsessed with food—especially his favorite, lasagna—Garfield the cat has been a star since 1978, when he first appeared in a comic strip drawn by Jim Davis. Today, the comic strip is still going strong; it appears in more than 2,500 newspapers worldwide. And Garfield himself has gone on to star in TV shows, video games, and movies. Davis created the character because he thought comic strips—while they featured a lot of dogs—lacked cat characters. And because Davis had grown up on a farm with 25 felines, he was the right cartoonist for the job.

SASSY
from *Homeward Bound*

Before the Seaver family heads out for a vacation, they drop off their pets at a friend's ranch for safekeeping. But Chance, a silly American bulldog; Shadow, a wise golden retriever; and Sassy, a Himalayan (p. 190) who lived up to her name, aren't so sure about the whole arrangement. Worried their humans are gone for good, they take matters into their own paws and embark on a treacherous journey to find their way back home. Sassy was played by a cat named Tiki, who wasn't a professional "actress"; prior to the film she was a rescue whose owner trained her to do stunts on cue. What a cool cat!

TOM
from *Tom and Jerry*

Though he's clever, the scheming Tom never catches the mouse—Jerry—in this American cartoon series. From their 1940 debut in the short *Puss Gets the Boot,* the animated enemies were a hit with audiences. They went on to star in nearly 150 episodes, some of which won Academy Awards, and their own movie. Even though the two critters almost never spoke, they kept viewers endlessly entertained as they quarreled, darted around, and generally annoyed each other. The series ran for decades, with Tom never getting tired of setting traps for his foe—which usually backfired, to the amusement of both Jerry and the show's fans.

SHORT, STUMPY TAIL

ROUNDED RUMP

ROUND-TIPPED EARS

ROUND HEAD

STURDY BODY

HEAVY LEGS

MANX

People once thought that these tailless cats were "cabbits"—the offspring of a cat and a rabbit. Today, people know that it's impossible to cross two different species, but there's no question how the legend came about. With its rounded rump, long back legs, and pom-pom tail, Manx cats definitely look a little bit like bunnies.

That's not the only legend about the origins of the Manx. One story says it was late to climb on Noah's ark, the biblical boat said to have saved all of Earth's animals during a great flood. The cat was the last animal to board, and as Noah closed the door for the last time, he caught the Manx's tail in the door, leaving it forever shortened.

What is known is that the Manx is a very old breed with a long history. Like the Kurilian bobtail (p. 98), the Manx originates from an island. Manx cats come from the small Isle of Man, which lies in the Irish Sea between Ireland and England. Sailors who were docked off the coast first noticed tailless cats living there in the 16th century. When the first tailless cat was born long ago—its missing tail was the result of a genetic mutation—the gene spread throughout the entire population of cats on the Isle of Man. This is why unique species like the Manx often come from islands.

Manx cats have been extremely popular since the early 20th century. It was their unusual appearance that first caught the attention of breeders, but it's their personality that makes them lasting favorites. Manx are fun-loving animals who make wonderful pets. They're often called doglike for their playful, loyal, and sweet personalities. They love to retrieve and will bring you something to throw over and over—even when you're trying to read or watch TV.

CAT STATS

FROM: United Kingdom
SIZE: 8–12 pounds (3.5–5.5 kg)
COAT: All colors, shades, and patterns
GROOMING:
CATTITUDE: Intelligent and loyal

Manx cats make friends with the family dog.

Manx cats will often choose one person to form a special bond with, but most love all members of their family. Since they're so devoted to their loved ones, they're not always the friendliest cats with strangers, preferring to keep their distance until they learn who the newcomer is. Manx cats are a great choice for families with children; they are usually patient with tiny humans who pull their ears and tails or squeeze them too tightly. And they don't get attached only to their human family; they also get along particularly well with the family dog.

The two creatures will often play games of chase, giving the humans in the family a spectacle to laugh at.

Most Manx are not loud cats. They like to communicate with chirps, trills, purrs, and head bumps. They are dignified creatures who will gracefully curl up in your lap if invited. But they're also active goofballs who will sometimes race around the room for no reason. Manx cats' owners say that their cats are loyal members of the family who can always be counted on to keep life interesting.

Manx have front legs shorter than their back legs, causing a **RABBITLIKE WALK**— sometimes called the **MANX HOP.**

WEDGE-
SHAPED HEAD

TAIL CAN BE
AS LONG AS
THE BODY

ROUNDED
CHEST

DENSE
COAT

LEGS ABOUT HALF
THE LENGTH OF
OTHER CATS' LEGS

MUNCHKIN

With its short legs and belly that nearly brushes the ground, this cat might remind you of a dachshund dog. It's called a munchkin, and it gets its stature from a natural genetic mutation. The munchkin is a relatively new breed that only appeared in the 1980s, but the gene that gives it its shortened legs has been around much longer than that: Reports of feral cats with stubby limbs date back to the 1930s.

The modern munchkin breed got its start when a Louisiana music teacher named Sandra Hockendal rescued a pregnant cat with short legs. That cat's kittens had short legs, too, and soon Hockendal's home was overrun with these lowrider felines. Later, breeders crossed cats to purposely maintain this gene.

Unlike some other cats with genetic mutations, munchkins are very healthy. The gene that gives them short legs doesn't appear to make them prone to disease or reduce their life span. In fact, munchkins are extremely active cats. They can move and dart so fast that it's hard to tell that their legs are any different from the average cat's. They might not be able to jump as high as their long-legged cousins, but munchkin cats can run, climb, and play—and they love to do it.

Though this breed hasn't been around for long, it has quickly won a place in the hearts of many cat lovers. Waiting lists for this adorable, quirky cat companion can be long.

CAT STATS

FROM: United States
SIZE: 8–12 pounds (3.5–5.5 kg)
COAT: All colors, shades, and patterns
GROOMING:
CATTITUDE: Intelligent and loyal

Many of these funny felines **LOVE TO STEAL SMALL OBJECTS** and stash them away for later.

OCICAT

If you're looking for a jungle cat look-alike that also loves to curl up in your lap, the ocicat might be the right breed for you. Despite its name and its wild appearance, the ocicat is not a cross between a domestic cat and an ocelot, the native cat that leaps through the jungles of Central and South America. The exotic-looking breed was actually an accident.

The first ocicat—then just a little ocikitten—was born in 1964 to Siamese (p. 138) and Abyssinian (p. 28) parents. Most of the kittens looked like a mix of their parents—except for one. The breeder's daughter remarked that the odd, spotted kitten looked like an ocelot, and asked, "Can we call him an ocicat?" Little did she know she had just named a new breed.

The family named that first ocicat Tonga and kept him as a pet, but his brothers and sisters went on to found the new breed. Later, breeders added American shorthairs (p. 34) to the ocicat lineage, making ocicats a little stronger and stouter. Cat enthusiasts have long been intrigued by the spotted coats of wild cats. But the ocicat was the first time they had attempted to create a cat with this wild look entirely from domestic cats.

ALMOND-SHAPED EYES

"NECKLACE" PATTERN

🐾 CAT STATS

FROM: United States

SIZE: 6–14 pounds (2–6 kg)

COAT: Black, brown, blue, lilac, and fawn in spotted pattern

GROOMING:

CATTITUDE: Loving and sociable

Some ocicat owners have trained their pet to **WALK ON A LEASH!**

ATHLETIC BODY

LONG TAIL

Ocicats are happier when they have companionship.

Ocicats feel heavy for their size. That's because they're extremely muscular, and those muscles make them a very athletic breed. Their dramatic coats are covered with thumbprint-shaped spots that contrast dramatically with the coat's background color. Ocicats come in 12 colors, but the most common are tawny, chocolate, and cinnamon. A distinctive "necklace" pattern around the neck adds to the ocicat's wild appearance.

Even though they look like they'd be at home prowling a jungle, ocicats actually love living in homes with their beloved human companions. Like dogs, ocicats are completely devoted to their people. Ocicats are highly social and usually not a good choice if they're going to be left alone often. But they thrive with companions, whether they're human, feline, or canine. Even when visitors come over, the family ocicat isn't shy about coming around to say hello—and if it decides the new person is worthy, the ocicat might even invite itself to take a nap in his or her lap.

ORIENTAL
SHORTHAIR

During World War II, many of Britain's cat breeding programs were shut down. Though the Siamese (p. 138) is an ancient breed that has been known in Thailand for centuries, their breeding stock in Britain was almost wiped out because so many breeding programs had been devastated by the war.

To keep the Siamese bloodline from disappearing completely, breeders began mixing in all kinds of other breeds, from Russian blues (p. 124) to Abyssinians (p. 28) to British shorthairs (p. 50). The result was a new breed, the Oriental shorthair, which now comes in more than 300 colors and patterns—more than any other breed.

Oriental shorthairs come in nine basic colors: white, red, cream, ebony, blue, chestnut, lavender, cinnamon, and fawn. And there are so many patterns and shades on top of that, these cats really do seem to come in all colors of the rainbow. They can have a silver undercoat, dark-tipped hairs, dramatic stripes, and paint splashes of red or cream. They even come in a long-haired version (p. 216).

But it's not just the Oriental's coat that makes this cat interesting. These cats form extremely close bonds with their people—they're practically attached to their owners at the hip! They'll help you pick your clothes out in the morning, keep you company while you brush your teeth, and rub against your legs while you eat your breakfast.

The Oriental's curious and social nature can some-times make these felines little rascals. They might nosedive into a purse to steal a favorite pen or empty a drawer to get at a chasable piece of paper. But for the owners of these funny, affectionate cats, their antics are all in good fun!

CAT STATS

FROM: United Kingdom

SIZE: 9–14 pounds (4–6.5 kg)

COAT: All colors, shades, and patterns

GROOMING:

CATTITUDE: Playful and people-oriented

HIND LEGS LONGER THAN FORELEGS

LARGE EARS

SLANTING EYES

LONG NECK

SLENDER LEGS

Oriental shorthairs come in so many colors that they're **NICKNAMED "RAINBOW CATS."**

CATS ON THE
CUTTING EDGE

Mr. Whiskers might be a good cuddle companion ... but did you know he's also the subject of serious scientific study? In recent years, experts have peered into cat DNA and have made all kinds of discoveries about everything from the origins of cat diseases to how felines went from being wild animals to our closest friends. Read on to learn about some of the most exciting new research on cat genetics.

GENETICS 101

Living things store information in molecules inside their cells. These molecules are called DNA. DNA is a long strand made of a sequence of four kinds of molecules. The order of this sequence acts like a set of instructions that tells our bodies how to develop and function. By figuring out the order, or "sequencing" the DNA, scientists can figure out how living things are made. In 2015, a team of scientists lead by geneticist—and cat lover—Leslie Lyons of the University of Missouri in Columbia, Missouri, U.S.A., set out to sequence the genomes of 99 domestic cats.

THE FIRST CAT to have its genes analyzed was an Abyssinian (p. 28) named Cinnamon, in 2007.

DECODING DISEASE

By sequencing the cat genome, scientists hoped to discover the genes that cause certain feline diseases—and develop more effective medicines. In 2017, researchers were able to identify a genetic mutation that causes blindness in an endangered species called the African black-footed cat. This knowledge will help breeding programs carefully cross captive black-footed cats to avoid passing on the mutation.

But this research doesn't just help cats. The same gene that leads to blindness in cats is known to cause vision problems in humans, too. It's one of many genetic disorders that are similar in both cats and people. Studying the feline genome may someday help experts better treat human diseases, too.

THE DNA OF DOMESTICATION

Scientists have also used DNA analysis to study the origins of cat domestication. In 2014, they compared the DNA of wild kitties with that of their couch-dwelling counterparts. They discovered mutations in three areas of the cat genome that may have changed the personalities of cats so they became friendlier and less wild.

The researchers found that, compared with wild cats, domestic cats have more mutations on genes that modify aggressive behavior, form memories, and control the ability to learn. Researchers think wild cats with these traits would have been more likely to get along better with—and live closer to—humans. Cats with these "friendly" genes would have crossed with each other, passing on the traits to their offspring. After generations, the friendlier cats were different enough from their wild cousins to form a whole new species: *Felis catus*, the domestic house cat.

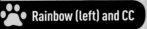
CAT CLONE

In 2001, scientists at Texas A&M University in College Station, Texas, U.S.A., cloned a pet for the first time. Scientists took DNA from a calico cat named Rainbow and transferred it into a feline egg cell. That cell became a new kitty named CC, short for Carbon Copy. But even though Rainbow and CC had identical DNA, the cats didn't look like exact copies of each other. Whereas Rainbow had a white coat with patches of brown, tan, and gold, CC had a striped gray coat over white. Rainbow was shy; CC was playful. Rainbow was a little chunky; CC was slim. What was going on?

Genetics are complicated—so complicated that, just because two creatures have identical genes, it doesn't mean they'll act or even look the same. That's because certain genes have to be activated, or turned on, to cause the traits they control to appear. The gene that controls the color orange in cats is one of these: If it's activated, the cat will have orange patches; if it's not, the cat will have black patches instead. Scientists don't yet completely understand what causes genes to activate and deactivate. Sometimes, it could be what happens while the kitten is in the womb or the environment it's raised in; other times, it could be random. But CC gave scientists a start in unraveling this genetic mystery.

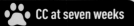
CC at seven weeks

MYSTERY OF THE TWO-FACED CAT

In 2012, an unusual-looking tortoiseshell cat named Venus became an internet sensation: She has a half-black, half-orange face with one green eye and one blue. She has three million followers on social media and has been featured on television shows and in commercials.

Venus's odd looks are a bit of a mystery even for scientists. It's a possibility that she's a chimera, an animal with two sets of DNA created when two embryos fuse together in the womb. Natural chimeras are extremely rare. But if Venus isn't one, then an unlikely series of genetic events led to her striking pattern. Genes causing orange fur could have been activated in all the cells on one side of her face, while genes causing black fur controlled the other side. Her blue eye is the biggest mystery: Usually only white-coated cats have baby blues, but Venus's only white fur is a small patch on her chest.

As Venus goes to show, the world of cat genetics is wildly complex, and scientists who study it still have many mysteries to explain. It's a good thing their subjects are so cute!

FELINE FAMILY TREE DECODED

Have you ever wondered where your cat came from? Maybe her ancestors walked through the misty forests of Norway, or maybe she can trace her lineage all the way back to the sacred cats of ancient Egypt. There's a way to find out for sure: Organizations such as the Veterinary Genetics Laboratory at the University of California, Davis, in California, U.S.A., can test your furry friend's DNA to find out if her parents or grandparents belong to some of the many recognized cat breeds. Interested owners can order a test, swab the inside of their cat's cheek to collect the DNA, and then send it to lab for analysis. Six to eight weeks later, they'll find out once and for all if their cat really is a rare Kurilian bobtail (p. 98) ... or just a look-alike.

PETERBALD

Lovers of the Peterbald often describe this cat as elegant and graceful. Others might call it, well … bald. Some Peterbalds are completely hairless; others have the downy covering of a peach or bristles like a man's beard. Their looks might seem a bit shocking at first, but their owners believe that if you give this unusual breed a chance, they will find their way into your heart.

Peterbalds are a relatively new breed. Breeders in the Russian city of St. Petersburg noticed that a kitten born in 1988 had an unusual coat. Excited, they thought they had discovered a cat with a dominant gene for a hairless coat—meaning that just one parent would have to carry the gene to pass it along to the kittens. Other bald cats, like the sphynx, carry baldness in a recessive gene, which means that both parents have to have the gene to pass it along. But the descendants of that first bald Russian kitty weren't always bald; many were born with hair, though their coats were not ordinary cat coats. The breeders realized that the original cat actually carried a gene for *hair loss*, not hairlessness. They named this unusual new feline the Peterbald.

A Peterbald will greet you at the door, jump in your lap whenever you sit down, sit by you for every meal, and sleep with you at night. If you're not looking for a cat that will stick to you like glue, the Peterbald might not be the right choice for you! But if you like the idea of a constant companion, this bald breed might just make the perfect feline friend.

KINKED WHISKERS

HAIRLESS OR NEARLY HAIRLESS COAT

🐾 CAT STATS

FROM: Russia

SIZE: 8–15 pounds (3.5–7 kg)

COAT: All colors, shades, and patterns

GROOMING:

CATTITUDE: Intelligent and affectionate

LONG HEAD

HUGE EARS

If going outdoors, a Peterbald will **NEED A SWEATER** in the winter and **FELINE-SAFE SUNBLOCK** in the summer.

LONG, THIN TAIL

THICK FUR
ABOVE EYES

BROWN-SPOTTED
TABBY FUR

BOBBED
TAIL

STURDY
BODY

SHORT COAT WITH
WOOLLY TEXTURE

PIXIEBOB

With its squinting eyes, broad chest, and stump of a tail, this cat might look like a fighter. But even though it's named after the wild mountain bobcat, this kitty is actually a purring ball of love that makes a great family pet.

The pixiebob's ancestry is shrouded in mystery. Many breeders think that it arose from the accidental crossing of a bobcat and a barn cat

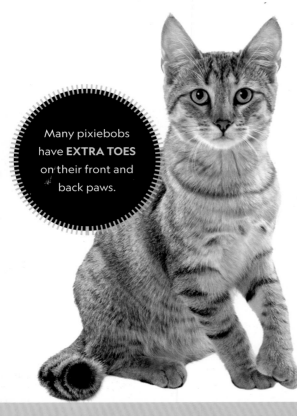

Many pixiebobs have **EXTRA TOES** on their front and back paws.

in the state of Washington, U.S.A. Their offspring, named Pixie, became the founding member of her new breed. Experts think the pixiebob probably isn't really related to the wild bobcat—but there's no doubt that it really does resemble a feral feline.

The pixiebob has tufted ears, a thick coat, and a strong body. These are big cats that can weigh up to 18 pounds (8 kg). Besides their wild appearance, pixiebobs have another odd trait: Almost half of all pixiebobs are polydactyls, which means they have extra toes. The average feline has five toes on the front paws and four in the back. Pixiebobs, on the other paw, can have as many as seven toes per foot—a total of 28 in all. This trait has been passed down from the very first pixiebob.

Some cat fanciers call the pixiebob a "dog in disguise" because this breed often acts more canine than feline. These intelligent, active cats can be taught to fetch and walk on a leash, and many love children and enjoy the company of other pets. So if you've always wanted a playful cat for a pal, the pixiebob may be the one for you.

CAT STATS

FROM: United States
SIZE: 9–18 pounds (4–8 kg)
COAT: Brown-spotted tabby only
GROOMING: 🖌🖌🖌🖌🖌
CATTITUDE: Good-natured and friendly

RUSSIAN BLUE

The first thing you might notice about these striking cats is their bluish gray coats. The second is their bright green eyes. Russian blues are renowned for their elegance and beauty, and they have been beloved for a very long time.

Experts believe that the Russian blue originated from the Archangel Isles in northern Russia. There is little written history about how these cats came to be, but there are many stories. Some say they rode into battle on the shoulders of their masters. Others say they were the companions of royalty. What is known is that the first Russian blue was exhibited at a cat show in 1875 at England's Crystal Palace. Today, they're a favorite at cat shows and among their devoted owners.

Russian blues walk on dainty, rounded paws, giving them the appearance of moving around on tiptoe like ballerinas. As fitting their elegant appearance, these cats are usually a little reserved and shy. But once they have been won over, they become loyal friends. They're highly affectionate with the people they love. Many Russian blues pick one particular person in the family to bond closely to. Once this striking, green-eyed cat has chosen you, you can be sure you've got a companion for life.

LONG BODY

LONG LEGS

 **CAT STATS**

FROM: Russia
SIZE: 7–12 pounds (3–5.5 kg)
COAT: Shades of blue
GROOMING:
CATTITUDE: Gentle and sweet

BRIGHT GREEN EYES

PLUSH COAT

Russian blues have thin, graceful bodies with **LONG LEGS AND TAILS.**

SMALL PAWS

SMALL HEAD WITH LARGE EARS

Savannahs are **ONE OF THE MOST EXPENSIVE** cat breeds, costing as much as **$20,000.**

LONG NECK

ATHLETIC BODY

VERY LONG LEGS

SAVANNAH

Most exotic-looking cats only *look* like they have wild ancestors. But not the Savannah. This breed actually is descended from the serval, a swift and powerful hunter that makes its home on the African savanna.

Savannahs originated from a chance crossing between a male African serval and a female domestic cat. One look at a Savannah and its wild ancestry is obvious: Like servals, Savannahs have long legs, huge ears that stand at the top of their heads, and a dark "tear" mark that extends from each eye, something that is common in wild cats like the cheetah. Savannah cats also inherited their spotted coat—which can come in a few colors, including brown, silver, and black—from the serval.

Looks aren't the only thing the Savannah got from its exotic ancestor. Servals are known for their jumping ability: They can leap up to eight feet (2.5 m) straight in the air. As Savannah cat owners know, that means these felines can jump from a standstill on the floor directly to the top of a door!

Savannahs are no lap cats. These intelligent, curious animals are constantly on the lookout for new entertainment, whether that means chasing a new cat toy or opening a cupboard and scattering the contents all over the house. They demand a lot of attention! But just because they have a lot of energy doesn't mean they don't make good pets for the right owner. These cats are loyal members of the family, and they love nothing more than playtime with their favorite humans.

ALERT EYES

CAT STATS

FROM: United States

SIZE: 12–22 pounds (5.5–10 kg)

COAT: Brown-spotted tabby, black silver-spotted tabby, or black smoke

GROOMING:

CATTITUDE: Curious and fun-loving

SCOTTISH FOLD

When people catch their first glimpse of a Scottish fold, with its teeny, turned-down ears and its huge, round eyes, they take a second look to make sure it's real. But this cat isn't a stuffed animal or a cartoon character—it's an actual breed descended from a Scottish farm cat.

The first Scottish fold was a white female with copper-colored eyes named Susie, who lived on a farm in Perthshire, Scotland. When a neighbor noticed the unusual-looking cat with the folded ears in 1961, he was intrigued. He and his wife asked for one of Susie's kittens, and they named the little female cat Snooks. Further crossings resulted in many more folded-eared kittens, and the Scottish fold became an official breed in 1974.

The Scottish fold's appearance can be described by one word: round. It has a round head with big, round eyes, and a round body with a puffy coat that only makes it look rounder. Then there are its ears: The result of a natural genetic mutation, they point downward and forward, making the cat's huge eyes look even bigger and giving it an innocent expression that many find irresistibly adorable. (The mutation can affect cartilage throughout the body and sometimes causes health problems as Scottish folds age. Because of this, the breed is controversial, and some say it should not be bred.)

CAT STATS

FROM: United States and United Kingdom

SIZE: 6–13 pounds (2.5–6 kg)

COAT: Most colors, shades, and patterns

GROOMING:

CATTITUDE: Sweet and quirky

DENSE COAT

ROUND BODY

FOLDED EARS

BROAD NOSE

SHORT
NECK

Scottish folds are the pet of choice for singing superstar **TAYLOR SWIFT.** She has two!

Even though the folded ears are the hallmark of the Scottish fold, not all of these cats have them. Some kittens grow up with straight ears, though they have the same chubby bodies and round eyes as their folded cousins. These cats, called Scottish straights (p. 132), still make great pets, and the breed can't go on without them, as Scottish fold kittens must have one parent with straight ears and one with folded ears. To keep from breeding unhealthy kittens, Scottish fold breeders must cross one Scottish fold parent with another Scottish straight parent. Each kitten from this crossing has a 50 percent chance of inheriting a copy of the ear-fold gene—but it's impossible for them to inherit the dangerous double copies.

Scottish folds are known for their loyal natures. They're sweet and playful, and they love attention. Their owners adore them for their funny habit of posing in odd positions: A Scottish fold might enjoy lying flat on the floor with its hind legs stretched out like a frog or balancing upright on its rear like a meerkat. They relish the company of people and get along well in all types of families. Because they're so social, they aren't the best choice for owners who will be absent often. But Scottish folds don't always need humans for company: They usually make friends with the family pets, too—though some other cats seem surprised the first time they see a fellow feline sporting folded ears.

As people fall in love with their adorable features and winning personality, Scottish folds are becoming more and more popular. But they are still a rare breed, and you're more likely to see one at a cat show than at a friend's house.

SCOTTISH STRAIGHT

Scottish straights are the brothers and sisters of Scottish folds (p. 128), but instead of ears that fold down as they age, theirs start out straight and stay that way. Half the kittens in a Scottish fold litter have folded ears, and the other half have straight ears. Some people choose to own one Scottish straight and one Scottish fold from the same litter—just for fun!

Scottish straights are medium-size cats with round bodies, round faces, and even round whisker pads, the area below a cat's nose from which whiskers sprout. Though their ears don't fold over, they are rounded at the tips, which makes the cat look all the rounder. These cats also have short legs and stout, almost chubby bodies.

These physical characteristics give them the look of stuffed animals. And, like Scottish folds, they love to hang out in weird positions. You might catch one sleeping in a patch of sun flat on its back with all four feet in the air.

Scottish folds get most of the attention, but Scottish straights are the same cat in a slightly different package. Despite their appearance, they're quite dexterous, and you might find yours slyly opening a cabinet door behind your back. They love toys, but the favorite plaything of a Scottish straight will always be its humans. They are great pets for families that want an affectionate cat. Scottish straights are gentle, making them a good choice for spirited children.

ROUND PAWS

CAT STATS

FROM: United States and United Kingdom

SIZE: 6–13 pounds (2.5–6 kg)

COAT: Most colors, shades, and patterns

GROOMING:

CATTITUDE: Sweet and quirky

STRAIGHT EARS

LARGE EYES

SHORT COAT

SHORT NECK

Scottish straights can usually be found **A FEW STEPS AWAY** from their people.

AMAZING
CAT STORIES

The following stories must be read to be believed! The five felines on these pages are fluffy and adorable— but they don't stop there. Among them are Millie, who rock climbs alongside her human; Dodger, who rides the city bus; and Sable, who made sure that students were safe while walking to school. These incredible stories of daring cats are hard to believe—but they're 100 percent true!

KULI THE SURFER

Surf the waves in Honolulu, Hawaii, U.S.A., and you might have an unusual companion on the water: a cat! Alex Gomez adopted this one-eyed cat as a tiny, one-pound (0.5-kg) kitten from a local animal shelter and named him Kuli. At first, it looked like the special-needs kitten might not make it. He threw up everything Gomez fed him and had to have baths twice a day to keep his fur clean. But Kuli rallied and grew stronger—and as a bonus, he was now used to water! Gomez, an avid surfer, wanted to see if Kuli would join her on the water. Over many trips to the beach, she gradually got him used to the ocean and the surfboard, and taught him how to swim so he would be safe if he ever fell. Today, Kuli is a pro surfer—he can even hang ten!

DODGER THE COMMUTER

When the X53 city bus in Bridport, Dorset, England, came to its stop, the passengers shuffled toward the door to climb aboard. First, a man carrying a shopping bag got on. Then came a lady in a purple jacket. Then, it was Dodger's turn. The orange tabby climbed the steps and then walked down the aisle, looking for an empty seat. It was clear to everyone watching that he knew the drill. That's because Dodger was a veteran bus rider who logged thousands of miles in his lifetime. His owner, Fee Jeans, worried at first, but as Dodger took trip after trip—always coming home again, she let him enjoy his life on the road. Passengers on Dodger's regular route grew to love their furry traveling buddy, who would gratefully eat the snacks they brought and sit on their laps, purring.

MILLIE THE ROCK-CLIMBER

Craig Armstrong of Salt Lake City, Utah, U.S.A., loves to rock climb—and so does his cat Millie! After many climbing trips, where he would watch other climbers with canine companions, he started thinking about a climbing buddy of his own. As a cat fan, Armstrong knew his buddy would have to be a feline. When Millie was a kitten, he got her used to the idea by hiking up hills. Not wanting to be left alone, Millie would scamper along. When he thought she was ready, Armstrong bought her a safety harness and took her outside, along with a friend and his own climbing cat. Today, the two human climbers let their cats roam free down canyons and across deserts, following them wherever they go—a new style of climbing they call catting.

SABLE THE CROSSING GUARD

Every weekday morning and afternoon, Sable would get up from his nap, stretch, and head to work. Luckily, his job was right across the street at Enterprise Middle School in West Richland, Washington, U.S.A. Sable had decided it was his job to be a crossing guard that helped the students make it safely across the busy street— and he took his volunteer position seriously. Sable would sit on the sidewalk and scan traffic, right next to the safety patrol station where a human crossing guard was doing the same thing. Sable knew better than to run into traffic, but when a student fell on the icy street, Sable leapt off his post and was the first on the scene. The school was so impressed that they made Sable an honorary safety patrol officer. Sable's owner bought him his own safety vest and would put it on the cat every morning. When Sable was on duty, not one child was ever injured crossing the street.

CURLY
WHISKERS

SHORT, SQUARE
MUZZLE

CURLY COAT

Most Selkirk
rexes LOVE
TO SNUGGLE.

MUSCULAR
BODY

LARGE
PAWS

SELKIRK REX

Sometimes called a "cat in sheep's clothing," the Selkirk rex has a wavy coat that looks like it should belong to a fuzzy lamb. Besides being nice to pet, Selkirk rex cats have clownish personalities that make them a favorite of many feline fanciers.

The Selkirk rex began with an unusual-looking kitten born in Montana, U.S.A., near the Selkirk Mountains. In 1986, a woman who ran a shelter out of her home took in a little calico cat that was missing a foot. Shortly after she was rescued, the calico gave birth to six kittens. One of them had a strange curly coat. Every hair on her body was curly, including the hairs on her tail and inside her ears! When this cat eventually gave birth to

her own litter and half the kittens had curly coats, her owner realized that this was the beginning of a brand-new breed.

Selkirk rexes' coats are made up of tightly packed ringlets, with most of the curls around the neck and belly. The coat is thick and plush, and it looks ready-made to be stroked at all times. The Selkirk rex has one odd characteristic—its curly whiskers, which are brittle and often break off into short little stubs. Even though cats use their whiskers to help them navigate at night, Selkirk rexes aren't missing out; because they grew up with short whiskers, they're used to getting around without them. These cats come in both a short- and long-haired (p. 236) variety.

Selkirk rexes have a silly streak that makes them hard to resist. They might climb up your back while you're bent over cleaning the floor or play peek-a-boo around the furniture. And almost all Selkirk rexes enjoy cuddling up to their people—a welcome attribute in a cat that feels like a teddy bear.

 **CAT STATS**

FROM: United States
SIZE: 7-11 pounds (3-5 kg)
COAT: All colors, shades, and patterns
GROOMING: 〰〰〰〰〰
CATTITUDE: Clownish and cuddly

SIAMESE

The Siamese is one of the oldest—and one of the most popular—cat breeds on Earth. Cats with light-color coats and black faces, ears, paws, and tails have been in Thailand (formerly called Siam) for hundreds of years. A book of Thai poems that possibly dates back to the 14th century tells of a cat in these colors called Maew Kaew. This "royal cat of Siam" has been captivating the cat world ever since.

Some legends say that Thai royalty kept the Siamese. Though this is indeed an aristocratic-looking cat, with its long limbs and elegant looks, the facts are less certain. What's known is that Siamese began appearing at cat shows in London in the 1870s. In the same decade, a Siamese was sent across the Atlantic to U.S. president Rutherford B. Hayes's wife as a gift. This breed captivated cat fanciers across the globe, and people began importing them in huge numbers. The first time a Siamese was awarded Best Cat in Show was in 1907.

CAT STATS

FROM: Thailand

SIZE: 6–12 pounds (2.5–5.5 kg)

COAT: All solid colors in pointed patterns

GROOMING:

CATTITUDE: Talkative and extroverted

FINE, SHORT FUR

LEAN, LONG BODY

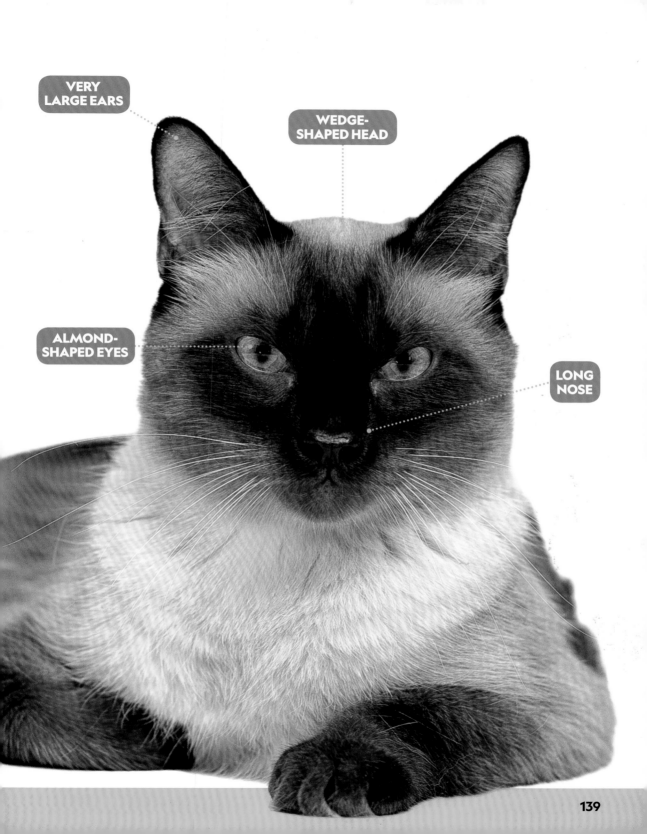

VERY
LARGE EARS

WEDGE-
SHAPED HEAD

ALMOND-
SHAPED EYES

LONG
NOSE

After that, the Siamese's popularity skyrocketed. Cat shows became more popular after World War II, and the Siamese and Persian cats (p. 220) dominated the winner's circle. Americans fell in love with the Siamese's unique color point markings, the result of a temperature-sensitive molecule that colors only the cool parts of the cat's body. Up until the early 1930s, all Siamese were seal points—cream with a chocolate brown face, paws, tail, and ears. Then new colors, like blue, chocolate, and lilac, were officially recognized by breeding organizations.

Before the 1970s, the Siamese looked more like the average shorthair than it does today, with an apple-shaped head and broad body. Breeders decided to go for a new look, and the modern Siamese has an angular wedge-shaped head, an elongated body, and very large pointed ears. They also have bright blue almond-shaped eyes that stand out in their dark faces.

The Siamese's unique color may have been what caught the attention of breeders, but it's this cat's personality that makes so many cat owners big fans. Siamese love human interaction: They consider it their duty to help you with whatever tasks you're doing and will lie on your computer keyboard, sit in your lap, and definitely sleep in your bed. They have a loud voice and they're not afraid to use it, demanding attention and love from the people around them. Some say the Siamese are the most outgoing of all cat breeds.

Many Siamese owners report that their cats are very good at figuring out how to **TWIST KNOBS TO OPEN DOORS.**

This breed is considered a **LIVING NATIONAL TREASURE** by the government of Singapore.

SMALL BODY

BARRING ON LEGS

STRONG LEGS

SINGAPURA

If you fall for this cat, you might have to join a waiting list to get a kitten: the Singapura, (the Malaysian word for Singapore, this cat's birthplace) is one of the rarest breeds in the world. They're small in stature—some weighing in at just four pounds (2 kg)—but Singapuras have big personalities.

The Singapura got its start when the small, delicate cat won the attention of an American scientist named Hal Meadow while he was working in Singapore in the 1970s. When he and his wife returned to the United States, they brought three kittens with them—named Ticle, Tes, and Puss'e—that became the founding members of the new breed. In 1988, the Singapura was accepted to compete in cat shows, and by the 1990s, British breeders had begun taking an interest in the cat.

Singapuras are slender, delicate-looking cats—but they have muscular bodies and long, strong legs. They have a short, silky coat that doesn't need much care, a slender body, and huge eyes that give them an angelic look. But don't be fooled—these are mischievous, fun-loving cats that know how to use charm to get exactly what they want. They wield their exceptional intelligence to playfully steal your pens or view the world from the vantage point of your shoulder. But they're sensitive, too, and one of their favorite places is under the covers in their favorite humans' bed.

CAT STATS

FROM: Singapore
SIZE: 4–9 pounds (2–4 kg)
COAT: Sepia agouti, seal brown ticking on ivory ground color
GROOMING:
CATTITUDE: Playful and intelligent

SLENDER TAIL

DARK MARKINGS ON CHEEKBONES

SNOWSHOE

All snowshoe cats have four white paws, the trait that gives them their name. Photographs of Siamese cats with this same feature date back the Victorian era, but the modern snowshoe was not developed until the 1950s. It was then that a Siamese breeder named Dorothy Hinds-Daugherty decided to create a Siamese-like cat with white feet.

Daugherty started with three white-pawed Siamese kittens and crossed them with an American shorthair that also had white paws. The modern snowshoe has a mix of characteristics from these two breeds. They have a long, athletic body, a short coat, and a rounded, slightly wedge-shaped head with striking walnut-shaped blue eyes.

The snowshoe is very smart, just like both its parent breeds. These cats like to learn tricks, and some can even be taught to run feline agility courses. They enjoy playing with running water, and a few snowshoes even like swimming. They love to be where they can observe the action, and their athletic bodies let them leap high, too—don't be surprised if you find your snowshoe up high in a bookshelf!

Like their Siamese descendants, most snowshoes love to "talk." In a soft voice, they'll seem to tell you all about their day and ask you about yours. Snowshoes are social cats that love their people, but they also get along well with other pets. They like company, and if their human family is gone all day, they'll often make special friends with another cat or the family dog.

LONG BODY

CAT STATS

FROM: United States

SIZE: 6–12 pounds (2.5–5.5 kg)

COAT: Typical Siamese colors with white feet

GROOMING:

CATTITUDE: Intelligent and social

OVAL PAWS

WALNUT-SHAPED BLUE EYES

HIGH CHEEKBONES

Snowshoes have an **EASYGOING PERSONALITY** that makes them a great choice for first-time cat owners.

WHITE SOCKS ON ALL FOUR FEET

SPHYNX

Some love it. Others think it looks like a wrinkled alien. All agree, however, that the sphynx is one of the world's most unusual cats. The breed may not appeal to everyone, but those who love these kitties say that their intelligent, affectionate personalities make them the best cats around—fur or no fur.

The best-known of all the hairless cat breeds, the sphynx isn't actually completely bald; most have a thin fuzz of hair covering their bodies, with more hair on their heads, tails, and paws. Don't get a sphynx if you don't like attention—this cat earns stares with its huge, batlike ears, rounded belly, and wrinkled skin.

Despite the fact that it's hairless, the sphynx comes from the cold, northern country of Canada. In fact, it's the only naturally occurring Canadian cat breed. In 1966, a farm cat in Toronto gave birth to a hairless kitten. The unusual trait was due to a natural mutation, making this cat the first member of a new breed. Along with several other hairless cats from around the world—one famously named Epidermis, the medical term for skin—this cat and its ancestors were crossed with both hairless and normal-coated cats. It took breeders about 30 years of careful crossing to develop the modern sphynx breed.

VERY LARGE EARS

CAT STATS

FROM: Canada

SIZE: 8–15 pounds (3.5–7 kg)

COAT: All colors, shades, and patterns

GROOMING:

CATTITUDE: Affectionate and intelligent

WRINKLED SKIN ON HEAD AND SHOULDERS

NEARLY HAIRLESS COAT

PROMINENT CHEEKBONES

Because furless felines can become sunburned even in the shade or on overcast days, sphynx cats should be **ALLOWED OUTSIDE ONLY UNDER CONSTANT SUPERVISION.**

ROUNDED BELLY

THE SKIN OF A SPHYNX IS VERY LOOSE, contributing to its wrinkly look.

The sphynx hairlessness gene is recessive. That means that when a sphynx is crossed with a normal-coated cat, all the kittens will have a normal coat. But when one of those kittens grows up and is bred to a sphynx, 50 percent of the kittens will be hairless.

Because of their lack of fur, sphynx cats do get cold easily. Many owners delight in outfitting their bare buddies in cute sweaters. But sphynxes are smart at keeping warm on their own, too—they'll always find the toastiest place to curl up. Sometimes that's next to a heater or cuddled up to the family dog, but most often their preferred location is in their owner's lap. And even though they don't have a coat to speak of, sphynx cats need regular grooming: Oils that would usually be absorbed into a cat's fur collect on the skin, so sphynxes must have regular baths.

The sphynx doesn't just snuggle close when it's cold. This is a highly social and affectionate cat that will follow you everywhere and likes to always be the center of attention. When strangers come over, the sphynx might hop onto their shoulders and perch there, purring—which can be quite a shock if the person wasn't expecting a hairless cat. Sphynxes are also very intelligent and enjoy getting into mischief, like opening cupboards and stealing human food. They get along well with dogs and other cats, but humans are always this unique cat's very favorite companions.

CATS IN SPACE:
THE STORY OF THE WORLD'S FIRST ASTROCAT

Space cats in training

In 1957, the Soviet Union launched a dog named Laika into Earth's orbit—the first ever animal to make the trip. Four years later, a brave chimp named Ham returned safely to Earth after his own historic spaceflight for NASA, famously greeting the captain of his recovery ship with a calm handshake. These astro-animals paved the way for the first humans to travel to space, and they're still famous for their flights today. But not many know the forgotten story of one fearless feline who blasted off into space on October 18, 1963.

MEOW MIX-UP

In the 1960s, the United States and the Soviet Union were leading the race to space. France had fallen behind, and it wanted to make its mark in the push to travel beyond Earth. It was going to do that by sending the world's first feline into space.

By 1963, the French had about 14 cats training for spaceflight. They spun in centrifuges to ready their bodies for the extreme g-forces of takeoff and tested out compression chambers that would help their bodies adjust to the pressure changes of space walks. One cat, named Félix, was chosen as the champion candidate.

But when launch day came, Félix disappeared. Apparently not eager to shoot into space at thousands of miles an hour, he escaped from the training center and was never seen again. Luckily, there was a brave feline to step into his place: a tuxedo-patterned kitty named Félicette.

STREET CAT TO SPACE CADET

Félicette began her life as a stray roaming the streets of Paris. But she was destined to go to great heights. On October 18, 1963, she boarded the research rocket Véronique AGI 47. She blasted off, successfully left Earth's atmosphere, and entered outer space. Her flight reached 130 miles (209 km) above Earth and lasted 15 minutes.

The mission completed, the capsule carrying the cat separated from the rocket, a parachute unfurled, and Félicette floated gently back to land. After her safe arrival, French scientists studied her brain waves, recorded during the flight. Little is known about what they learned, but the experts stated that the little space cat made "a valuable contribution to research."

Despite the success, France was left behind in the space race. The Soviet Union had already sent the first human to orbit Earth, Yuri Gagarin, in 1961, and the United States would later become the first nation to land men on the moon, in 1969. So the story of the brave black-and-white kitty was mostly forgotten. Even so, Félicette deserves a place in the history books as the world's first *cat*ronaut.

POINTS ON EARS AND FACE

ALMOND-SHAPED BLUE EYES

LONG BODY

SHORT COAT

Some say that living with these smart and fun-loving goofballs is like **LIVING WITH TODDLERS.**

POINTS ON FEET AND TAIL

THAI

In the 1970s, breeders of the Siamese (p. 138), a cat originally from Thailand, began to alter that cat's looks to give it the long body and triangle-shaped head the breed is known for today. But before those changes, the original Siamese looked much more like this cat—called the Thai.

The Thai people have cherished a light-colored cat with dark legs, head, ears, and tail for at least 700 years. Descriptions of this cat, which the Thais call Wichienmaat, appear in ancient Thai texts. Western breeders wanted to create a more extreme and striking version of this cat, and the result was the modern Siamese, with its extremely blue eyes, long body, and sharply angular head. Many people loved the changes to the Siamese—but not all. And beginning in the 1950s, those who loved the traditional look set out to preserve it in the Thai.

Thais share the personalities that make the Siamese such popular pets. They follow you around the house, "helping" you out with your chores, chatting away the whole time with their expressive voices. When meows won't cut it, they also use body language—like tapping you with a paw or putting their face nose-to-nose with yours—to get a point across. These cats aren't the best option for people who want a pet that can entertain itself. But for those who want a close feline friend, the breed may be the ideal choice.

🐾 CAT STATS

FROM: Thailand
SIZE: 6-12 pounds (2.5-5.5 kg)
COAT: All solid colors in pointed patterns
GROOMING: 🐾🐾
CATTITUDE: Talkative and extroverted

LONG, TAPERING TAIL

TONKINESE

Created by crossing Siamese (p. 138) and Burmese (p. 58) cats, the Tonkinese brings together the best of both breeds. It has beautiful coloring set off by bright, greenish yellow eyes, a rich coat, and an independent but loving personality. It's no wonder that the Tonkinese is a popular cat breed in both the United States and the United Kingdom.

Siamese and Burmese were first crossed in the 1950s by American cat breeder Milan Greer, who called the cats "golden Siamese." Other breeders took up the idea, interested in creating a cat with the affectionate nature and intelligence of the Siamese but with a quieter meow.

The breed wasn't widely recognized until the 1970s, but once it was introduced to the show ring, it catapulted into fame. There have been many Tonkinese Grand Champion cats since then.

Tonkinese are known for their intelligent, outgoing personalities. They love humans and seem to be convinced that all humans love them back. They consider their rightful place to be on your lap or shoulder, and they think it's their duty to supervise all your activities. They're not the most trainable of cats, but their owners love their smart and sassy personalities. Like their Siamese cousins, Tonkinese are extremely talkative. When it wakes up from a nap, this cat will run through the house, calling its owner until the human responds.

SLEEK COAT

CAT STATS

FROM: United States

SIZE: 6-12 pounds (2.5-5.5 kg)

COAT: All colors except cinnamon and fawn, in many patterns

GROOMING:

CATTITUDE: Loving and independent

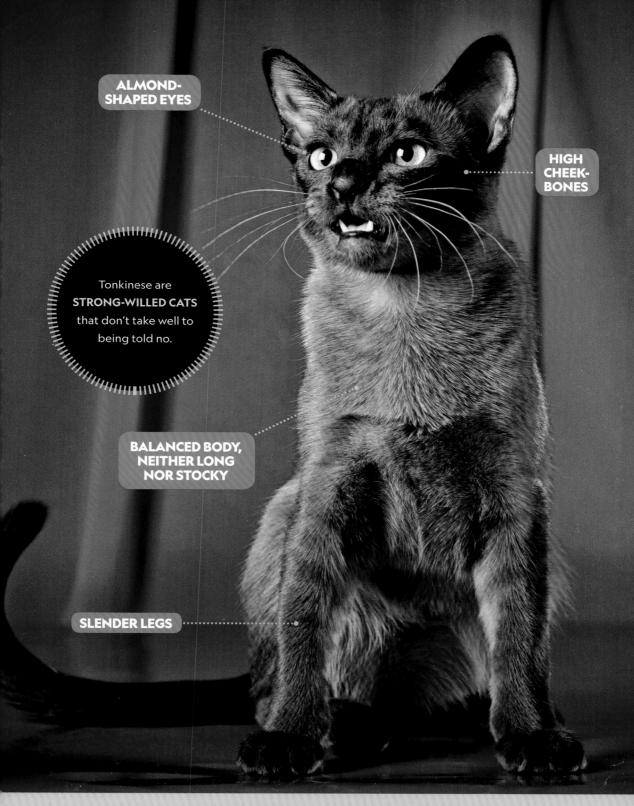

ALMOND-
SHAPED EYES

HIGH
CHEEK-
BONES

Tonkinese are
STRONG-WILLED CATS
that don't take well to
being told no.

BALANCED BODY,
NEITHER LONG
NOR STOCKY

SLENDER LEGS

TOYGER

With its striking stripes and lean, muscular body, the toyger looks every bit the toy-size version of the tiger it's named for. A "designer" cat bred to resemble the jungle-dweller, the toyger has a coat patterned with bold vertical stripes on an orange-tinted background. But even though it looks like a wild animal, the toyger doesn't behave like one. This is a relaxed and affectionate cat that makes a great pet.

The toyger got its start in the 1980s with a breeder named Judy Sudgen. Previously devoted to the Bengal (p. 44), a breed that her cat-breeder mother founded, Sudgen decided to cross one of her prized felines with a tabby domestic shorthair. When she noticed spots on one of the kittens, she set her sights on developing the exotic-looking new breed. The toyger was officially recognized in 2007.

When it started appearing in show rings, the toyger's dramatic looks made people sit up and take notice. The cat even appeared on the cover of *Life* magazine in 2007, along with an article that called the toyger "America's next superpet." But raising a house-size jungle cat comes at a price: Toygers can cost up to $5,000, so they're not the ideal choice for everyone. Fortunately, some of the expense is for a good cause: Many toyger breeders donate a portion of their proceeds to wild tiger conservation programs.

CAT STATS

FROM: United States
SIZE: 12–22 pounds (5.5–10 kg)
COAT: Brown mackerel tabby only
GROOMING:
CATTITUDE: Relaxed and friendly

The toyger is **ONE OF THE NEWEST CAT BREEDS.**

LONG, MUSCULAR BODY

SPOTTED TABBY COAT

SPOTS HAVE VARIOUS SHAPES, LIKE ROUND, BLOCKED, AND OVAL

EARS SET HIGH ON HEAD

TAIL HAS DARK TIP

They may look like tigers, but toygers are actually laid-back, friendly felines.

Toygers have long, strong bodies that they carry low to the ground, in the manner of wild cats stalking prey. Also like tigers, they have extra-long toes and powerful paws. Their short but dense coat is often said to glitter like it's dusted in gold.

Toygers are exceptionally friendly cats that love the company of people. They're very intelligent, and owners report that they're highly trainable and easy to teach to walk on a leash. These cats are active and athletic, but that doesn't make them hard to handle; their easy-going attitude makes them beloved pets of many people looking to add a little piece of the jungle to their lives.

HOW TO
SPEAK
CAT

When you get home, your kitty is waiting at the door. She chirps and chitters, then rubs her face against your legs, purring loudly. It seems like she's trying to tell you something ... but what?

Cats may not speak, but that doesn't mean they don't communicate. Like many other animals, felines use sounds and body language—like the position of their eyelids or tails—to get their point across. And even though Fluffy will never learn human language, that doesn't mean you can't learn how to communicate with her. Read the pointers in the next few pages, and you'll be speaking cat in no time!

FACE TO FACE

In the wild, cats may live in groups, but they are very independent. If they reveal what they're thinking, they could give a competing cat the upper paw. So cats' faces don't give away much—sometimes just a glance or a blink. But if you know what to look for, that can be enough to get a sense of what's on their mind.

THE STARE

You've probably been in a staring contest with another person—but have you ever gone eyeball-to-eyeball with a cat? Felines are staring contest masters, but it's more than a game for them. Cats use staring to show their dominance; you might notice the behavior when one neighborhood kitty encounters another he doesn't like. So it's best not to stare a cat directly in the eyes. It's only natural that they consider it threatening.

THE SQUINT

If you've ever caught your cat with eyes squeezed tight, you might think he looks angry. But it's more likely he's just wearing the cat version of sunglasses. Cats' eyes are easily damaged by strong sunlight. Luckily, they have several methods of sun protection: They can narrow their pupils or half-close their eyes to limit the light coming in.

THE SLOW BLINK

If a cat looks into your eyes and blinks slowly, feel flattered—you've just been offered the ultimate sign of friendship. A slow blink means that the cat likes being with you. Even if she looks away right after, consider it a compliment—she's totally relaxed around you and feels so safe that she doesn't need to stay on alert. So next time you're hanging out with your cat, share the love and give her a slow blink—if you're lucky, she'll do it right back.

EAR SIGNALS

It's tough for humans to judge a cat's mood from the position of its ears—after all, we don't use *our* ears to communicate. But cats do. When a cat is relaxed, her ears will be on standby: standing up and facing forward or slightly to the sides. Stiff ears mean she's on alert, possibly focused on potential prey. Twitching ears mean she's nervous. Sideways ears mean she's annoyed (or she's just monitoring the sounds around her—watch carefully to tell the difference), and flattened ears mean she's full-on angry (stay away!).

WHISKER TALK

Whiskers aren't just cute: They are an essential part of how your cat senses the world. When a cat's whiskers are pointed forward, that means he's alert. That's because when he hunts in the dark, he fans his whiskers out and sweeps them along in front of his body. When the whiskers detect the vibrations made by prey—*wham!*—he pounces. But beware of whiskers pointed backward: They mean a cat is angry or afraid. That's because cats pull their whiskers against their faces to protect them during fights.

TAIL TALES

A cat's tail can have as many as 23 bones and make up one-third of its spine. Tails help cats counterbalance so that they can stay upright when turning a tight corner, climbing a tree, or even just jumping on the couch. But tails have another function, too: Cats use them to communicate. But it wasn't always so. Long ago, when cats were solitary forest-dwellers, they didn't use their tails to signal their mood. This ability evolved only after cats moved into human settlements. Suddenly in the company of other cats, they had to learn how to speak to each other and get along. Here's what their tails are telling.

POINTED UP

This tail position means a cat is happy and relaxed. A cat holds her tail high to signal to another feline that she's friendly. If she does it as she approaches you, she wants to say "hi."

CURVED UP

Kittens spend most of their days playing. That's because the pouncing and rolling is preparing them to be hunters. But sometimes the playing gets too rough: If a kitten wants to stop, he signals this by arching his back, curling his tail up, and jumping straight into the air.

POOFED UP

This is one tail signal that's straightforward. Cats fluff out their tails when they're ready for a fight. When they're in an aggressive situation, adrenaline floods their bodies, making all their hair stand on end. That helps the cat look big and scary in the hopes that he'll intimidate his opponent into walking away before things get physical.

WRAPPED AROUND

A cat with its tail wrapped around its body can be tough to interpret. If she's calm, with eyes closing and ears relaxed, she's just curled up for a nap. But a cat with wary eyes and ears with a tail wrapped around her body is like a human with his arms crossed in front of his chest—it means your cat feels uncomfortable and wants others to keep their distance.

TWINING

When two cats from the same family group greet each other, they hold their tails up and twine them together. It's the cat way of showing love and affection. But they don't just use this signal with other cats: If your cat walks up to you and twines her tail around your leg, you've received the equivalent of a kitty hug.

TWITCHING, THUMPING, AND WAGGING

These tail signals are for expert-level cat communicators. It can be tough to tell the difference between them, so pay attention to your cat's other body language signals, too. A twitching tail can mean a cat is uneasy—or that she's in hunting mode. A thrashing tail often means a cat is frustrated. And experts can't agree on what a wagging tail means—some think it's a sign of anger, others think it means indecision. Each cat is different, so watch and learn your cat's unique signals; over time, you'll learn to read what she's trying to say.

165

CAT NOISES

Did you know that adult cats usually meow only at humans? Kittens meow to their mother to let her know they need a comforting cuddle or a drink of milk, but cats rarely use their voices with each other. With their humans, however, it's a different story: Cats meow, chirp, and chitter, among many other types of vocalizations. Experts think that's probably because cats learn at a young age that meowing helps them get what they want from people. Good thing they sound so cute!

MEOWING

Meows are the most common noise cats use to "chat" with you. They have a whole range of these noises—from high-pitched chirps to long, loud *mrrOOWWs*. Every cat uses these noises a bit differently, so pay attention to your own cat's unique meows. She might make a series of chirps when she's happy to see you when you get home and a loud meow when she's hungry. If you pay attention and listen closely, you'll learn your cat's personal "language."

CHATTERING

You might hear this odd noise from a cat who's in the house, watching birds flap around outside. Ears forward, tail swishing, your cat chatters his teeth together while focused intently on the birds. He's frustrated by the food that he can't reach—imagine how you would feel if someone was holding an ice-cream cone just out of your grasp!

PURRING

Kitties have a lot of adorable attributes. But purring probably ranks number one; this sweet, soothing sound makes us feel happy and content. However, purring doesn't always mean your cat is content, too. Cats make this sound, which comes from vibrating muscles in the voice box, when they're happy, but also when they're sick, injured, or stressed. Experts now think that cats could use purring to signal that they're in need of company. So next time you hear your kitty purring, go curl up with her—it'll make you both feel good.

YOWLING

Most cat noises are pleasant to listen to. But not yowls. These loud noises will jolt you awake in the middle of the night—they sound like something out of a scary movie. Cats yowl when they're angry, disoriented, or in pain. Fighting cats yowl back and forth in a deafening duet, called caterwauling, until one attacks.

HISSING

You probably already know that cats hiss when they're angry. But there's more to this snakelike sound: Cats use it as a warning signal—often along with a warning growl—when trying to scare another cat or a predator away before a fight breaks out. Sometimes they even spit!

Sometimes, a cat makes a face similar to the one he uses while hissing, but no sound comes out. Cats have a special structure in the roof of their mouths called a vomeronasal organ, which allows cats to sense smells in the air around them. When a cat is using this organ, she opens her mouth and pulls back her upper lip, exposing her teeth. But she's not angry—she's just taking everything in.

LONG-HAIRS

Long ago, all cats had short coats. But one day—maybe in a cold mountain region or deep in a chilly forest— a kitten was born with longer-than-normal hair.

Her fur coat kept her warm in the winter, and she grew up to be a strong and healthy cat mother of kittens who were long-haired just like her. It's thought that long hair in domestic cats came from this kind of natural genetic mutation. Longhair breeds first showed up in western Europe in the 16th century, and people immediately thought they were the cat's pajamas. Today, long-haired coats of all types, from smooth and silky to fluffy and puffy, are beloved by cat owners around the world.

ALERT
EXPRESSION

LARGE,
DEEP-SET
EYES

The American
bobtail's athletic air
gives this cat a **WILD
APPEARANCE.**

MUSCULAR
BODY

SHORT,
CURVED
TAIL

HEAVY
LEGS

AMERICAN BOBTAIL

If you spot an American bobtail when you're not expecting one, you'd be forgiven for thinking a bobcat has wandered into the house. These cats, with their substantial bodies, furry coats, and short puffs for tails, look like untamed forest-dwellers. But they're simply the beloved breed called the American bobtail.

Before European explorers docked their ships off the coast in the 15th century, there were no known domestic cats on the North American continent. But bobtailed cats have been known for centuries to live on the islands of Spain and Portugal. No one knows exactly when, but it's likely that one of these cats came over to the new land as a stowaway. After an adventure at sea spent keeping the ship's rodent population under control, this cat sauntered off the gangway into a whole new world.

American bobtails come in both a short-haired (p. 32) and a long-haired version. The bobtail long-hair is a large, powerfully built cat with a muscled body. Its athletic air gives it a truly wild appearance. Unlike the Manx (p. 104), the bobtail's tail isn't missing, just shortened—most are between one and four inches (2.5–10 cm) long. When the bobtail is standing, its tail is clearly visible above its back. It's not unusual for long-tailed kittens to be born alongside short-tailed littermates.

This breed has a calm personality and usually gets along well in busy households or quiet ones. They welcome visitors, make friends with dogs, and don't mind being carried around by young children—even if they sometimes get squeezed a little too tightly. They love shiny objects, so cabinets and jewelry boxes have to be kept closed from their prying paws. Bobtails are notorious clowns and often goof off to make their owners laugh. No wonder people who own bobtails are totally devoted to the breed.

CAT STATS

FROM: United States
SIZE: 7–15 pounds (3–7 kg)
COAT: All colors, shades, and patterns
GROOMING:
CATTITUDE: Loving and gentle

AMERICAN CURL LONGHAIR

The story of this cat with the unusual curling ears began on a summer day in June of 1981.

When Joe Ruga came home from work, he noticed two stray kittens outside his house. His wife, Grace, went out to feed the babies and noticed that they had an unusual appearance—their ears curled back, away from their heads. Though one kitten disappeared, the other, named Shulamith, grew up to be a member of the Ruga family—and the first ever American curl.

At first, the Rugas just saw Shulamith as a pet. But soon they realized that her curled ears might mean she was an entirely new breed. They had her genetically tested and found that, indeed, Shulamith's curled ears were the result of a spontaneous—and never-before-seen— mutation. The Rugas set about breeding more curls, and today this cat is considered one of the newest breeds with unusual features.

An American curl's ears can point back in a 90-degree curve or curl totally backward in a 180-degree bend. When the kittens are born, their ears are straight, but after a few days, they begin to change shape, reaching their full arc by the time the kitten is about four months old. The American curl's coat is fine and silky to the touch, with very little undercoat, which makes grooming easy. Curls have a long, plumed tail that waves as they walk.

CAT STATS

FROM: United States

SIZE: 7–11 pounds (3–5 kg)

COAT: All solid colors and shades, patterns include colorpoint, tabby, and tortie

GROOMING:

CATTITUDE: Affectionate and gentle

LONG, PLUMED TAIL

The curl's looks might get it noticed, but its character is what makes its owners such fans. These felines have big personalities: They like to watch TV, sleep in the fruit bowl, and play in water whenever they can. They follow their own- ers everywhere and think they're great helpers when you're making dinner or cleaning up. They keep kitten-like traits into adulthood and often tear through the house after a favorite toy, making their owners smile in delight.

EARS CURL BACKWARD

ROUNDED MUZZLE

An American curl's ears can point back in a **90-DEGREE CURVE OR CURL TOTALLY BACKWARD** in a 180-degree bend.

FINE COAT

STRONG YET SLENDER BODY

TOP 5
COOLEST
CATS
IN CHILDREN'S BOOKS

With their silent slinking and habit of coming out after dark, cats have a mysterious air. Maybe that's why the world's most famous literary felines often seem to have a little something magical about them. From the Cat in the Hat to Aslan the Lion, these famous felines put a whiskered face on many book covers—and became characters beloved the world over.

THE CAT IN THE HAT
from *The Cat in the Hat*

Before *The Cat in the Hat,* children were taught to read from books that were meant just to educate—not to entertain. Kids had a hard time paying attention, making it more difficult for them to learn how to read. So William Spaulding, the director of book publisher Houghton Mifflin's education division, challenged Dr. Seuss (the pen name of writer Theodor Geisel) to write something so fun to read that kids wouldn't be able to put it down. But there was a catch: He could only choose from a list of 250 simple words. Dr. Seuss rose to the challenge with his tale of a mischievous cat who entertains two children while their mother is away. The world fell in love, and today, the book has sold more than 11 million copies in 26 languages—and changed the way kids learn to read forever.

THE CAT IN THE HAT

THE CAT IN THE HAT Dr. Seuss

THE CAT IN THE HAT

I CAN READ IT ALL BY MYSELF
Beginner Books

By Dr. Seuss

MRS. TABITHA TWITCHIT
from the Beatrix Potter books

Author Beatrix Potter is best known for her children's books starring animal characters like Peter Rabbit, Jeremy Fisher, and Jemima Puddle-Duck. But she was also an amateur scientist: Though proper ladies in the Victorian era didn't go to college, Potter collected fossils, examined archaeological artifacts, and most of all, studied the living things around her. The animals at her countryside home in northwest England inspired many of her most beloved book characters, like Mrs. Tabitha Twitchit, the long-suffering mother cat who tries—unsuccessfully—to keep three unruly kittens clean while preparing for proper guests to come for tea.

MR. MISTOFFELEES
from *Old Possum's Book of Practical Cats*

Cats, the story of a tribe of singing and dancing cats, is one of the most famous musicals of all time: The Broadway production ran for 18 years and won numerous awards. But many lovers of the now-classic stage performance don't realize that the show is based on a book of poems called *Old Possum's Book of Practical Cats.* Lifelong cat lover T. S. Eliot wrote the rhymes as gifts for the children of his friends, adapting traditional children's verses to tell a whimsical story about cats like Mr. Mistoffelees, a magician and mischief-maker. Little did he know his cat-centric poems would go on to make history.

KIRJAVA
from *His Dark Materials*

Author Philip Pullman made his mark on literature when he published his award-winning trilogy of fantasy novels called *His Dark Materials* from 1995 to 2000. To date, more than 17.5 million copies of the books have been sold. The books tell the story of two children as they travel through a series of parallel universes. In the world of main characters Lyra Belacqua and Will Parry, every human has a daemon, an animal that represents their inner spirit. Will's daemon takes the form of a smoke-gray cat named Kirjava. Kirjava gets separated from Will and goes on to have an adventure of her own, but, like any loyal daemon—or pet cat—she's always there for Will when he needs her most.

ASLAN
from *The Chronicles of Narnia*

He's not a pet cat, but Aslan is perhaps the most famous feline in all of literature. This talking lion is a main character in C. S. Lewis's seven-novel series *The Chronicles of Narnia.* At the same time frightening and comforting, mysterious and wise, Aslan rules his subjects with a benevolent paw, and all creatures in his kingdom worship him. At the beginning of *The Lion, the Witch, and the Wardrobe,* the first book published in the series, Aslan has been absent for many years. The evil White Witch has taken over and turns his loyal followers one by one into stone. Everyone expects Aslan to vanquish the villain upon his return ... and that's as much as we can say without revealing any spoilers!

WEDGE-SHAPED HEAD

DEEP BLUE EYES

It is believed that a Balinese can **SENSE THE MOOD OF ITS HUMAN.**

BALINESE

If you love the Siamese but have your heart set on a long-haired cat, you're in luck. The Balinese is a long-haired version of the Siamese, and they have the same energy, curiosity, and talkative nature as their cousins—just covered with a fluffy coat!

The origins of the Balinese are mysterious; no one knows exactly how or where this cat came to be. Most experts think it probably arose from a spontaneous mutation of the Siamese that resulted in a longer coat. Records show that Siamese litters included long-haired kittens as early as 1900. At first, they were seen as Siamese unfit for the show ring, and they were placed in homes as pets. But in the 1940s, people realized that these kitties were worthy of their own breed. By 1975, a Balinese had earned Grand Champion status.

Balinese have a long, fine, silky coat that comes in four colors: seal point, chocolate point, blue point, and lilac point. They have a wedge-shaped head, large ears, and eyes so deep blue that they really stand out.

This breed is so friendly and sociable that they want to do everything their humans do, from sitting on the couch and watching TV to sleeping under the covers at night. And they have energy to burn—you'll tire of playing fetch long before your Balinese will. They love to "talk," and when you get home, they'll greet you at the door and "tell" you all about their day.

POINTED COAT

LONG, STRONG BODY

LONG LEGS

CAT STATS

FROM: United States

SIZE: 6–11 pounds (2.5–5 kg)

COAT: Seal, chocolate, blue, and lilac self colorpoints

GROOMING:

CATTITUDE: Social and talkative

BIRMAN

Like the Balinese (p. 176), the Birman looks just like a long-haired Siamese. But the Birman isn't actually a Siamese relative. This color point cat has blue eyes, a luxurious coat, and a gentle, loving personality.

Legend says that Birmans owe their coloring to a cat that belonged to a priest in ancient Myanmar (once called Burma) who was attacked by robbers. When the robbers fled the temple, the Birman planted himself on the wounded priest's body. Touched by the cat's gentle gesture, the goddess of the temple granted the cat its gold-tinted coat and deep blue eyes, after her own appearance. His paws remained forever white where they had touched the priest.

Birman owners might agree that their cat has divine qualities. But experts think the likely true story is that the first Birman was bred in France in the 1920s from cats acquired in Myanmar. Careful crossings gave the breed its long coat, slightly curved nose, strong body, and full cheeks.

These cats are great middle-of-the-road pets—they're not as active as cats like the Abyssinian or as relaxed as the Persian. These easygoing felines are perfectly fine entertaining themselves for a while but will let their human know when attention is needed with a loud *meow*! They become lonely if left alone too often, but as long as they have a companion, they're happy.

Birmans love to have ANOTHER ANIMAL BUDDY.

CAT STATS

FROM: Myanmar and France
SIZE: 10–18 pounds (4.5–8 kg)
COAT: All color points, with white feet
GROOMING:
CATTITUDE: Gentle and easygoing

MEDIUM-
LENGTH TAIL

RUFF
AROUND
NECK

SILKY
COAT

ROMAN
NOSE

WHITE PAWS

BRITISH
LONGHAIR

With its chubby cheeks and sturdy body topped off with a fuzzy coat, the British longhair is the ultimate teddy bear cat. A long-haired cousin of the British shorthair, this is the perfect kitty for someone who wants the calm, people-loving temperament of that breed wrapped in an extra-huggable coat.

When the Romans invaded Great Britain centuries ago, cats imported from Egypt tagged along with the troops. Between 1914 and 1918, these cats were crossed with Persians (p. 220), which passed along their gene for long hair to some of the offspring. British shorthairs became popular in the show ring, but the occasional long-haired kitten wasn't seen as anything special, and many were given away as pets. That changed in the past few decades, when breeders began to sit up and notice them as worthy of their own breed. The International Cat Association awarded British longhairs Championship status in 2009, but some organizations still don't recognize these cats as a separate breed.

British longhairs can come in almost any color but are often found in unusual tones such as gray, cream, and rust not often seen in other breeds. Other than their coat, they look very similar to their British shorthair cousins, with a squarer skull and more prominent forehead.

British longhairs are affectionate cats that don't demand attention, but they do enjoy it. Males tend to be more easygoing, whereas females are more reserved. These aren't especially active cats, and they prefer to spend their days relaxing and calmly observing their kingdoms. These felines are usually happy to amuse themselves, and they don't need people or pets around all the time to keep themselves happy.

🐾 CAT STATS

FROM: United Kingdom
SIZE: 9–18 pounds (4–8 kg)
COAT: Nearly all colors, shades, and patterns
GROOMING:
CATTITUDE: Relaxed and easygoing

SHORT, BROAD NOSE

MEDIUM-LONG COAT

SHORT BACK

British longhairs have a medium-length, **VERY DENSE COAT** that gives them a plush appearance.

LONG "BRITCHES" OR FUR ON HINDQUARTERS

LARGE PAWS

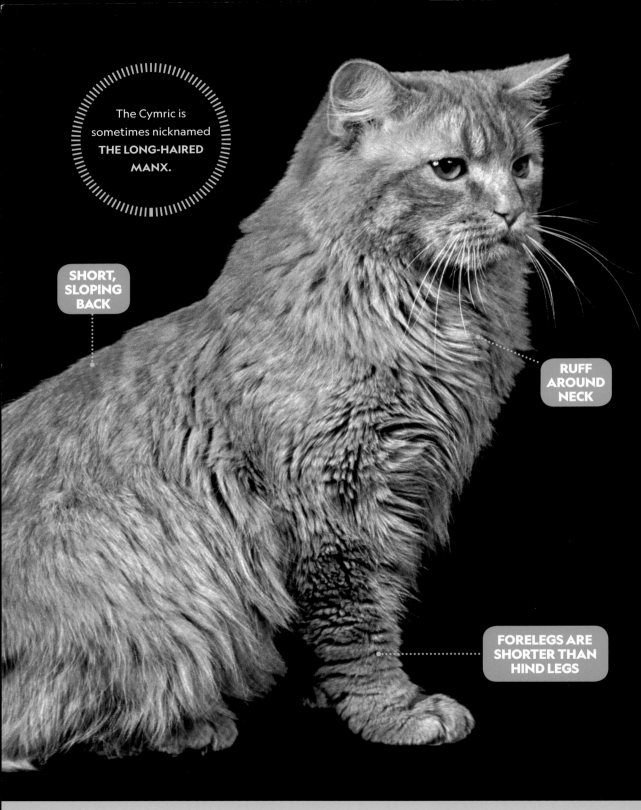

The Cymric is sometimes nicknamed **THE LONG-HAIRED MANX.**

SHORT, SLOPING BACK

RUFF AROUND NECK

FORELEGS ARE SHORTER THAN HIND LEGS

CYMRIC

If the Cymric reminds you of a long-haired version of the Manx (p. 104), you're right on: The only difference between the two cats is the length of their coats. These intelligent, happy cats aren't just striking in appearance; they're also loyal and lovable pets known to form close attachments with their human family.

The Manx cat is an old breed, and its origins are more legend than fact. Tailless cats were first spotted on the Isle of Man in the 16th century when sailors docked there. There are many stories of how these cats lost their tails. One claims the first tailless cat was shipwrecked on the Isle and became the ancestor of all Manx and Cymrics. What is known about this breed's beginnings is that the short-haired Manx was first recognized by the Cat Fanciers' Association in the 1920s. In 1989 the Cymric got official status, too.

The Cymric, whose name derives from the Welsh name for Wales, has a long, flowing coat that includes extra fluff on the hind legs (nicknamed "britches") and around its neck (called a ruff). Even though its lack of a tail is the most standout characteristic of the breed, not all of these cats are completely missing their tails. Many have one or two tail vertebrae that give them a small nub.

Manx and Cymrics look a little different, but the two breeds share a personality: They love to have fun. These are cats that will bring back objects to be thrown for them, carry toys around in their mouths, and chase the family dog around the house. Unlike most cats, they're known to love water, and if their house has a dripping sink, it's a good bet that's where the Cymric will be.

CAT STATS

FROM: North America
SIZE: 8–12 pounds (3.5–5.5 kg)
COAT: All colors, shades, and patterns
GROOMING:
CATTITUDE: Fun-loving

TAILLESS

BRITCHES ON HIND LEGS

TOP 10
WILD CATS

Not all cats love to sit in your lap. While years of cross-breeding have given us the domestic cats we know and love, it's the will to survive that has shaped wild cats. These fierce felines prowl jungles, grasslands, and deserts around the world. They use their smarts and speed to outwit other predators, and they're some of the most incredible animals on the planet.

AFRICAN GOLDEN CAT
(Caracal aurata)

This cat is so rare that it wasn't until 2015 that researchers captured the first ever photographs of its kittens. These cats live in central and west Africa, are about twice the size of a house cat, and are incredibly secretive: Almost everything about them is a mystery.

BOBCAT
(Lynx rufus)

When spotted in the wild, they're often mistaken for domestic cats, but bobcats are anything but. These wild felines, named for their short "bobbed" tails, are the most widely distributed cat in North America, even living in big cities like Los Angeles—but U.S. residents would hardly know it: Bobcats are so shy and elusive that most people have never seen one.

IBERIAN LYNX
(Lynx pardinus)

One of the world's most endangered cat species, wild Iberian lynx numbered fewer than 100 in 2002. Hunting by humans, habitat loss, and epidemics that have devastated the population of their main food source, rabbits, brought them to the brink of extinction. Since then, their numbers have tripled thanks to programs that breed the cats in captivity, raise the kittens, and release them back into the wild.

PALLAS'S CAT
(Otocolobus manul)

With its extreme fluffiness, the Pallas's cat looks like an adorable stuffed animal. But its fur, the longest and densest of any cat's, has a function: It helps keep this cat warm in the snow and frozen ground of its homeland in the mountains of central Asia.

MARBLED CAT
(Pardofelis marmorata)

Another incredibly rare cat, this feline lives in Southeast Asia. It's one of the least understood cats in the world: All that's known about it comes from one scientific study of a single marbled cat in Thailand. Here's what we do know: They probably use their incredibly long, bushy tails for balance, and they can turn their feet backward to help them climb trees.

BLACK-FOOTED CAT
(Felis nigripes)

The smallest cat in Africa, this feline can weigh as little as 2.5 pounds (1.13 kg). It is found in deserts and savannas, where it stalks small rodents, birds, and insects by night. Its low-slung body is ideal for slinking though short grass without detection, and its small stature allows it to squeeze inside rabbit holes and even hollow termite mounds to escape the hot African sun during the day.

LEOPARD CAT
(Prionailurus bengalensis)

It's easy to see where a leopard cat gets its name: It looks exactly like a pint-size leopard. These wild kitties live in many habitats from jungles to semi-deserts across Southeast Asia and parts of India. Like its look-alike cousin, the leopard cat likes to spend its days resting in trees, emerging at night to hunt.

FISHING CAT
(Prionailurus viverrinus)

Your house cat might flee at the sound of the shower— but the wild fishing cat loves water. These felines live along rivers, streams, and in swamps and wetlands across South and Southeast Asia. They have webbing between their toes that helps them swim and also scoop prey like fish, crabs, crayfish, and frogs right out of the water.

JAGUARUNDI
(Puma yagouaroundi)

Looking more like a weasel than a cat, this unusual feline has a small, flattened head and a tail like an otter's. They live in southern North America and South America, surviving on rodents, rabbits, armadillos, opossums, reptiles, frogs, and fish. Experts believe that a small number of jaguarundis kept as pets in Florida escaped in the 1940s and began a small population still living there today.

SAND CAT
(Felis margarita)

If you saw a sand cat in the wild, you might think you'd just spotted a particularly cute kitten. With their huge ears, big eyes, and tiny noses, sand cats look kitten-like all their lives. They're the only felines in the world that make the desert their primary home. Their huge ears help release heat from their bodies, and their furry feet help protect them while walking on hot rocks and sand.

BIG CATS

They watch over the savannas of Africa and leap through the jungles of Asia. They're some of the world's top predators and among Earth's most impressive animals, including the mighty lion, the ferocious tiger, and the speedy cheetah—the fastest land animal. Sadly, big cats are at risk: Humans have hunted many species, and other big cats' habitats are disappearing as humans move in. Conservationists all over the world are working to protect these animals and make sure they still have a place on our planet.

LIONS

Nicknamed "King of the Jungle," these large predators rule their territories in sub-Saharan Africa. The only cats to live in groups, lions gather in "prides" of 15 or more animals. The male lion's job is to protect the rest of the pride. To scare off rivals, he greets each morning with roars that can be heard five miles (8 km) away. At up to 420 pounds (190 kg), he's really big—too big to be a deft hunter. That job is for the nimble lionesses, which work in teams to prey upon large animals like antelopes and wildebeest.

TIGERS

Tigers are the largest and most powerful of all the big cats. These fearsome hunters live alone, prowling many miles to track down buffalo, deer, wild pigs, and other large animals that live in their territory of India and Southeast Asia. Their stripes help camouflage tigers in their grassland and forest habitat, keeping them hidden so they can sneak up on unsuspecting prey. One pounce is usually all it takes for this powerful predator to triumph. Hungry tigers have been known to eat as much as 60 pounds (27 kg) of meat in a single night.

JAGUARS

Jaguars love to swim: They often paddle down rivers in their Central and South American homelands to hunt for fish, turtles, or small alligator-like animals called caimans. They also use their strong jaws and teeth—the most powerful of all cats—to attack larger animals like deer, capybaras, and tapirs. Most jaguars are orange with black spots, but some, called black jaguars, are so dark that it's hard to see their spots. These cats have a long history in Native American culture: They're considered symbols of strength and power and often linked with royalty.

LEOPARDS

Leopards are most comfortable in trees, where they spend their days dozing in the branches. At night, they'll yawn, stretch, and then leap to the ground for the hunt. If they're successful, they often drag their kill back up into a treetop to keep it safe from scavengers like hyenas. Leopards live in sub-Saharan Africa, northeast Africa, Central Asia, India, and China. Their distinctive spots help conceal their bodies as they slink through grass and forests. But they're not completely spotted: Each leopard has a white tip on the end of its tail that young cubs follow when they're mimicking mom to learn how to hunt. And, like jaguars, not all leopards are spotted: Some, called black panthers, can also appear all black.

CHEETAHS

Cheetahs are the fastest animals on land: They can go from zero to 60 miles an hour (97 km/h) in just three seconds—as fast as a sports car! They're sprinters, not marathon runners, so before they take off, cheetahs use their keen eyes to zero in on their target in the grass. A cheetah's small head, long legs, and slender body all contribute to its great speed. Its long tails acts like a rudder that helps it make sudden turns during a chase; that's how cheetahs outmaneuver expert runners like antelopes. Cheetahs live in eastern and southwestern Africa.

MOUNTAIN LIONS

This big cat goes by many names: mountain lion, cougar, catamount, panther, red tiger, deer tiger, and puma. Mountain lions can live in many kinds of habitats, and they have the widest geographic range of any land animal in the Western Hemisphere besides humans. Years ago, they roamed all over the United States, but today, the mountain lion is mostly seen in the western United States, where they survive mainly on deer. Fast movers, strong swimmers, and excellent climbers, mountain lions have powerful hind legs that allow them to leap as far as 45 feet (14 m).

SNOW LEOPARDS

High up in the mountains of Central Asia lives a rare and elusive cat: the snow leopard. These cats have large, furry feet that act like natural snowshoes, and thick, spotted gray coats that help keep them warm in their cold homeland. In summer, their fur is a yellowish gray color that blends in perfectly with the rocky mountains. But in winter, their coats turn off-white to conceal them in the snow. Snow leopards hunt small animals like hares and birds but can also bring down blue sheep and mountain ibex, animals that can be three times their weight.

CLOUDED LEOPARDS

One of the rarest big cats of all, the clouded leopard is almost never spotted in its homeland of Asia, where it lives from Indonesia to the Himalaya. These cats have short, powerful legs and rear ankles that rotate, making them exceptional climbers—they've even been spotted hanging upside-down beneath large branches! Scientists know very little about these elusive cats' habits in the wild, but they think they probably come down from the trees to hunt animals like deer, pigs, monkeys, birds, and squirrels. To help them hunt, clouded leopards deploy a powerful weapon—the largest canine teeth of any cat, relative to its body size.

HIMALAYAN

It took breeders more than a decade of careful crossings of Persians and Siamese cats to create the Himalayan, a long-haired cat with Siamese (p. 138) coloring. Known as the colorpoint Persian in the United Kingdom, this is a cat that has all the characteristics of its Persian (p. 220) relative, plus a lush fur coat in dramatic pointed patterns set off by bright blue eyes. This Persian in Siamese clothing is a cat that gets noticed.

Some official organizations recognize the Himalayan as its own breed; others say it's a variety of Persian. This cat was created in the 1950s when British and North American breeders decided they would try to produce a Persian with Siamese points.

The Himalayan—or Himmie for short—has a stocky body, round face, and short snub nose. The long, thick coat they are known for mats easily, so if you're looking for a cat that doesn't require much care, this isn't the breed for you: Experts say that daily grooming is a must to keep this cat tangle-free. The breed is also prone to excessive tearing and needs the corner of its eyes regularly wiped out. And litter can easily get lodged in its paws or coat, so Himalayans must have their bathroom areas kept spotlessly clean.

Like Persians, Himmies are sweet and gentle. They enjoy sitting quietly on the sofa and being petted by those who love them much more than they like climbing the furniture and breaking into cabinets. They are very affectionate, but they usually reserve their love for the people they know and trust. They like quiet homes, though they get along with children who don't tug their ears or force them into baby clothes. And Himalayans are happy to relax alone, making them a good choice for busy families.

CAT STATS

FROM: United States

SIZE: 8–15 pounds (3.5–7 kg)

COAT: Solid, colored, and tortie and tabby patterned points

GROOMING:

CATTITUDE: Gentle and sweet

BLUE EYES

SMALL EARS

LONG, THICK COAT

STOCKY BODY

They're more work than most cats, but **HIMMIES** are considered by their owners to be **MORE THAN WORTH IT.**

SHORT, FLUFFY TAIL

WIDE-SET EARS

The Japanese bobtail once **HELPED SAVE JAPAN'S SILK INDUSTRY** from rodents.

LARGE, OVAL EYES

LONG COAT PARTS ALONG SPINE

KINKED, SHORT TAIL

SLENDER LEGS

OVAL PAWS

JAPANESE BOBTAIL LONGHAIR

The Japanese people have long revered this native cat breed for its beauty. Japanese bobtails are pictured in silk screens and wood-block prints, usually along-side elegant ladies, dating back to the 16th and 17th centuries. Fanciers of this breed say that this furry cat with the tufted tail is a piece of living Japanese art.

Japanese bobtails come in both long-hair and short-hair (p. 90) versions. Experts aren't sure when the mutation that resulted in their distinctive short tails occurred. But since bobbed-tailed cats are common all over Asia, they think that this trait may date back to prehistoric times. Bobtails were probably brought to Japan from China or Korea in the sixth century and given the job of protecting royal manuscripts from mouse nibbles. Only members of the court owned these prized felines—until a rodent infestation put the nation's silk industry at risk. Royal decree ordered that all pet cats were to be released to the streets to help get a paw up on the problem. The silks were saved, but the refined, delicate bobtails of antiquity crossed with street and farm cats. The modern Japanese bobtail of today is heavier and larger than its ancient ancestors.

This breed is very high-energy and not for owners looking for a lounging lap cat; the Japanese bobtail is active, playful, and prone to mischief. Centuries of rodent-hunting made this breed smart and savvy, and it uses those traits to open cabinets, wiggle into boxes, and commandeer household objects as toys. If you're looking for an adventurous, lively feline friend who's always up for a romp, the Japanese bobtail might be the perfect pet.

🐾 CAT STATS

FROM: Japan

SIZE: 6–9 pounds (2.5–4 kg)

COAT: All solid colors in bicolor, tabby, and tortie patterns

GROOMING:

CATTITUDE: Lively and lovable

KURILIAN BOBTAIL LONGHAIR

The trademark of the Kurilian bobtail is its pom-pom tail. The tails are fuzzy, they're fluffy, and no two are exactly alike. Some tails are made of 10 vertebrae, and others are made of just two. Kurilian owners have names for each tail type, from "snag" to "spiral" to "whisk." But one thing's for sure—they love them all.

Kurilian bobtails are stocky, medium-size cats with large heads and bright gold eyes that get their name from the Kuril Islands in the North Pacific Ocean. Because both Russia and Japan claim these islands as their own, this cat has no true home country. Both the long-haired and short-haired (p. 98) Kurilian bobtails have been popular in Russia since the 1950s, but the breed is probably much older than that. It survived in its island home hunting and eating rodents—and some even say salmon!—on the Kuril Islands. But even though this cat looks wild, it loves the company of people and makes a great pet.

Kurilian bobtails are still rare outside of Russia, and especially rare in the United States. But its personality and looks are sure to change that. The Kurilian bobtail has a lush, silky coat; a broad, strong body; and of course, that poof of a bobbed tail. These cats have a kitten-like personality; they're playful and extremely friendly. They love visitors, dogs, and other cats, but above all, they love their humans. Kurilian bobtails are happy to entertain themselves, and a few daily head rubs will keep them happy members of the family.

CAT STATS

FROM: Kuril Islands, North Pacific
SIZE: 7–10 pounds (3–4.5 kg)
COAT: Most solid colors, shades, and patterns
GROOMING:
CATTITUDE: Playful and kitten-like

SHORT, KINKED TAIL

LARGE, ROUNDED HEAD

MEDIUM-SIZE EARS

OVAL EYES

A Kurilian bobtail's tail can be **RIGID OR FLEXIBLE, STRAIGHT OR KINKED** in any direction.

STOCKY BODY

PURR-FECTLY LUXURIOUS
CAT HOTELS

For some chic cats, a kennel simply isn't good enough. Felines are known to love the finer things in life, always seeking out the warmest, softest, coziest spot in the house. But these cat accommodations take their furry clients' comfort to the next level. Some offer room service, massages, and even TV just for kitties! All are paw-sitively five star.

DIVINE CREATURES
Australia

Feline guests of this hotel are in good hands: Every staff member is a trained veterinary nurse. Owners can choose among themed rooms that offer their kitties a taste of vacation destinations from Fiji to Paris. If they feel like getting some exercise, cats can take advantage of the hotel's play area; if they just want to wind down, they can tune into a specially created cat TV channel.

THE INGS LUXURY CAT HOTEL
United Kingdom

The Ings is truly one of the finest places for your favorite feline to relax while you're away. Instead of chocolate on their pillows, feline guests are greeted with a tempting treat of catnip. The hotel boasts spa treatments complete with aromatherapy, private balconies ideal for birdwatching, and big-screen televisions that play DVDs of cat-pleasing sights like swimming fish.

THE BARKLEY PET HOTEL AND DAY SPA
United States

It's not cats-only, but Fluffy won't mind having some doggie companions around when she learns about the luxury services available at this Los Angeles, California, cattery. While human guests stay at the Four Seasons hotel across the street, their pets can enjoy breakfast in bed or have a massage. Cats with discerning appetites can even dine on ahi tuna sushi from room service.

CATZONIA
Malaysia

Billed as the world's first five-star hotel for cats, this 35-room luxury inn in Kuala Lumpur offers a choice of four room categories, including VVIC (Very Very Important Cat), which rooms up to 10 felines and comes with three "king"-size beds and a playground.

LONGCROFT
United Kingdom

When cat lover Abi Purser couldn't find a place worthy of hosting her beloved cat, Norman, she decided to open one of her own. The result was Longcroft, a hotel that offers premium cat comfort. Guests catnap in wrought-iron beds set in individually decorated suites and dine on an organic à la cat menu developed by a feline nutritionist.

ALMOND-SHAPED EYES

BROAD MUZZLE

LONGEST CURLS ON RUFF

CURLY COAT

CURLY, PLUMED TAIL

These cats are best known for their **STRIKING CURLY COAT.**

LAPERM
LONGHAIR

Someone who happens upon a LaPerm kitten might be very surprised when it grows up to be an adult. Some LaPerm kittens are born hairless, but when they hit two weeks old, their coat starts to come in—and it's curly! This cat comes in both a short-haired (p. 100) and long-haired variety. The coats of short-haired LaPerms often stand on end like a bottle brush, but a long-haired LaPerm is a sight to behold: covered in lustrous curls, with a tail adorned in ringlets, and a full, curly ruff like a lion's mane.

LaPerms came from Oregon's Columbia River Gorge in the spring of 1982. A domestic barn cat gave birth to a litter of six kittens, one of which was completely bald. In addition to its lack of hair, it had large, batlike ears and skin that looked to be tattooed with a tabby pattern. By all accounts, it wasn't the most beautiful kitten, but its owner raised it lovingly, and by four months of age, the kitten had sprouted a full coat of cascading waves. The owner, Linda Koehl, named the cat Curly and thought nothing more about it until Curly gave birth to her own kittens—all as bald as she had been at birth. For the next 10 years, curly cats roamed Koehl's property. Eventually, she named the curly cats LaPerm, meaning "wavy" in several languages, and set to creating an official breed through careful crossings.

Underneath its rugged coat, the LaPerm is one graceful feline. Its long legs make it especially agile, so this is a breed that loves to play—though it's equally happy to sit in your lap and receive cuddles. They love people and affection: LaPerm kittens have been known to seek out the source of a human voice before their eyes have even opened. This is a cat that will lie contentedly over your shoulder or cradled in your arms as you walk around the house. And LaPerms are known for one unusual and adorable personality trait—their love of giving their humans frequent nose rubs!

CAT STATS

FROM: United States
SIZE: 8–11 pounds (3.5–5 kg)
COAT: All colors, shades, and patterns
GROOMING:
CATTITUDE: Active and affectionate

MAINE COON

This big cat with the long furry tail belongs to the first pedigreed cat breed native to the United States. Maine coons weigh an average of 9 to 17 pounds (4–7.5 kg)—though some males can tip the scales at more than 20 pounds (9 kg)! Maine coons are gentle giants who love nothing more than cuddling with their human family.

As its name hints, the Maine coon was originally spotted in the state of Maine, U.S.A. But how it got there is a mystery to this day. There are all kinds of legends about the origins of the Maine coon, each one more fantastical than the last. One tale tells of a French sea captain named Samuel Clough, who was tasked with smuggling Marie Antoinette—a French queen who had fallen out of favor with her people—out of the country. Captain Clough outfitted his ship with all the luxurious furniture and decorations the queen was accustomed to—including her six cats. Before the queen could board her escape vessel, she was beheaded—but Captain Clough escaped with her possessions and her cats. Those cats crossed with American cats to create the Maine coon.

Another story says an English captain named Coon used to sail up and down the coast of Maine with a crew of long-haired cats along for the ride. When the captain docked and went ashore, his cats came along. When long-haired kittens started popping up in Maine, people would call them "one of Coon's cats." Some legends are even wilder than that: One tells that the Maine coon arose when some of the domestic cats of Maine crossed with wild raccoons!

CAT STATS

FROM: United States

SIZE: 9–17 pounds (4–7.5 kg)

COAT: Many solid colors and shades in tortie, tabby, and bicolor patterns

GROOMING:

CATTITUDE: Gentle and loving

TUFTED EARS

LONG, THICK TAIL

SQUARE
MUZZLE

LARGE,
STURDY
BODY

LARGE,
ROUND FEET

Maine coons
are **ONE OF THE
BIGGEST BREEDS.**

Maine coons probably aren't descended from royal felines, and they certainly can't claim a raccoon as a great-grandparent (although their big bushy tail does look a bit like those of the masked mammal). They probably came from long-haired cats brought back to the coastal state of Maine by sailors who picked up feline friends on their world travels. Those cats crossed with the local shorthairs who came to the area in the company of American settlers, and the Maine coon was born.

The Maine coon was originally prized for its rodent-catching skills, and these cats have a water-resistant coat that's handy for hunting on damp days. It looks heavy and shaggy, and it's short on the shoulders and long along the stomach and back legs. These cats have large, tufted ears and oval eyes the color of copper.

The Maine coon's lovable personality has made it a favorite cat breed for decades. Often described as doglike, they're gentle giants that usually get along well with children and dogs—even though they can sometimes be bigger than Fido. Maine coons are happy enjoying their own company and like to pass the time watching birds and, of course, taking long naps. But when the family is home, the Maine coon is never far away and can be found in the kitchen during dinner or on the couch when it's movie night.

SMALL EARS

SHORT
MUZZLE

Minuet cats
are a cross between
the **MUNCHKIN**
and the **PERSIAN.**

SHORT LEGS

MINUET

 This short-legged cat is also called the Napoleon, after the supposedly short-statured French dictator Napoleon Bonaparte (who historians now know actually wasn't so short after all). Legend has it that Napoleon himself was actually afraid of cats, but it's hard to believe he couldn't love this kitty, with its big-eyed, doll-like face and adorably low-slung body.

The minuet gets its short legs from munchkin (p. 108) ancestors, and its luxurious coat from Persians (p. 220). Though most cats have just one hair for each follicle, Persians and minuets can have up to six hairs in a single follicle. That makes its coat especially fluffy and plush. Unlike Persians, minuets don't have a squashed face—making the minuet cat free of the breathing problems that can plague its Persian relatives. The minuet has a round head with big saucer eyes that stare up at its human begging for a pat. It has a dense coat and a compact, muscular body that sits atop its short legs. It unusual stature doesn't interfere with its physical ability: Minuets are active cats that can sprint through the house on their short legs just as well as their long-legged cousins.

Like their Persian cousins, minuets were born to be lap cats. They love people and like to be around them at all times. Though they might look sweet and innocent, these cats have a playful side, and their antics keep their owners laughing. But when they're tired out from playing, the minuet can always be counted on to curl up in your lap and purr itself to sleep.

LONG, PLUMED TAIL

CAT STATS

FROM: United States

SIZE: 7–17 pounds (3–7.5 kg)

COAT: All colors, shades, and patterns

GROOMING:

CATTITUDE: Playful and affectionate

SEMI-LONG COAT

CATS OF THE PAST

Millions of years ago, many catlike creatures prowled Earth. Some looked like modern cats, but others were bigger and fiercer than any feline alive today. Fossils show that the most ancient cat ancestors lived during the Eocene epoch, about 50 million years ago. Check out a few of Earth's most amazing extinct cats—and be thankful you don't have to worry about running into one today!

SMILODON

These are the most famous of all the extinct felines ... and for good reason. Larger than a modern tiger, this saber-toothed cat, nicknamed the "saber-toothed tiger," was one of the most dangerous predators of the Pleistocene epoch (the time period that spanned from about 2.6 million to 11,700 years ago). *Smilodon* would linger in the treetops, waiting for an unsuspecting animal to wander underneath. When it did, this ferocious feline would drop onto its prey's back and use its daggerlike 11-inch (28-cm) teeth to deliver a fatal blow. This technique—and those terrible teeth—allowed *Smilodon* to take down huge herbivores like ancient relatives of camels and bison. *Smilodon* was so fierce that it's the only known animal in history (other than humans) to have caused the extinction of another creature: a marsupial known as *Thylacosmilus*.

XENOSMILUS

A relative of *Smilodon*, this cat had shorter chompers that at first don't seem as impressive as its saber-toothed cousin's. That is—until you realize that *Xenosmilus*'s teeth had serrated (sawlike) edges, giving it the deceptively cute nickname "the cookie cutter cat." Like a shark's teeth, these were meant to slice through flesh, and they made this cat one terrifying predator: It didn't chase after its prey like the modern cheetah, ambush it like a leopard, or deliver a killing bite like *Smilodon*. Instead, it tore a chunk out of its victim and simply waited for its life to end. Then, *gulp*.

HOMOTHERIUM

Lions may be the modern-day kings of the jungle, but for five million years, *Homotherium* ruled, well, just about everything. This cat adapted to a whole variety of habitats and lived across North and South America, Europe, Asia, and Africa. Fossil remains found in the North Sea suggest that these cats could reach 882 pounds (400 kg). And if that's not scary enough, unlike most modern big cats, *Homotherium* hunted in packs. Some paleontologists believe they worked together to take down woolly mammoths.

CAVE LION

This ancient beast got its name from the many cave paintings that depicted it. No doubt the prehistoric artists feared—and perhaps even worshipped—this animal: Cave lions were truly gigantic, weighing up to 661 pounds (300 kg), making them about a third bigger than modern lions. But they didn't look much like lions of today: Besides the size difference, cave paintings show that the cave lion had no mane and perhaps also sported stripes on its legs and tail. Cave lions prowled the woodlands and mountains of Eurasia during the late Pleistocene epoch and went extinct only about 14,000 years ago.

AMERICAN LION

You read that correctly—lions once roamed North and South America. And they were the largest known cat ever to have lived, weighing as much as 1,102 pounds (500 kg)—as big as a horse! In fact, they were one of the most massive animals of their time, second only to the giant prehistoric bear *Arctodus simus*. The first American lion fossil was found in the La Brea Tar Pits, pools of muck located in modern Los Angeles, California, that trapped many ancient animals passing by. Like modern lions, the American lion probably lived a solitary life on the open grasslands of its ancient homeland during the Pleistocene epoch, which spanned 1.8 million to 11,500 years ago.

MUNCHKIN
LONGHAIR

If you thought this short-legged cat would be better suited to taking naps than racing around the house, you'd be wrong. The munchkin is built low to the ground—just like a race car. It's a speedster breed that loves to zip around in top gear. Its agility makes this cat a great playmate and a fun pet.

Munchkins have become popular in recent years, but they're not new on the scene. Short-legged cats have been recorded for decades in all corners of the globe. One British veterinary report even followed four generations of a munchkin family. The gene that results in these cats' short legs is a natural mutation, and unlike some short-legged dogs, such as the dachshund, munchkins don't have spinal problems. The munchkin was awarded Championship status by the International Cat Association in 2003.

ALERT EXPRESSION

CAT STATS

FROM: United States

SIZE: 6–9 pounds (2.5–4 kg)

COAT: All colors, shades, and patterns

GROOMING:

CATTITUDE: Playful and social

Munchkins come in both a short-haired (p. 108) and long-haired version, and in almost any color that can occur in a cat. Munchkin longhairs have a semi-long, silky coat that fares well in all kinds of weather. It must be groomed regularly to keep it from matting, but a quick combing a few times a week is all it takes. These cats have flat foreheads, rounded ears, and muscular bodies tipped with a rounded tail the same length as their body.

These cats have playful personalities and adore owners who will indulge them in a game of chase or pull a string for them to pounce on. These curious cats are known to investigate bags left on the floor and every open shelf; they even like to perch on their hind legs like a rabbit to get a better view.

LONG TAIL

FURRY BRITCHES

MUNCHKINS ARE VERY SOCIAL and love the company of adults, children, and other pets alike.

WEATHER-RESISTANT COAT

SHORT LEGS

LARGE
EARS

YELLOWISH
GREEN EYES

FEATHERING
BEHIND EARS

Like the mist they
were named for,
these shy creatures
tend to FADE INTO
THE BACKGROUND.

BLUE
COAT

HAIR TUFTS
BETWEEN TOES

NEBELUNG

In German, this cat's name means "creature of the mist," and, indeed, the nebelung's silvery blue coat does remind one of an overcast morning. The nebelung was created as a throwback cat meant to mimic long-haired cats popular in Victorian times.

The nebelung got its start in Denver, Colorado, U.S.A, in the late 20th century. Breeder Cora Cobb had a black domestic shorthair female and a long-haired black male produce a litter. One kitten in the bunch was long-haired, its coat an unusual blue color. The kitten captured Cobb's interest, and she named him Siegfried. Another litter from the same parents produced another long-haired blue kitten, this one a female Cobb named Brunhilde. Siegfried and Brunhilde became the parents of a new breeding program. Later, Russian blues (p. 124) that carried the gene for long hair were crossed into the line, and the new breed was fully recognized in 1997.

All nebelungs have greenish yellow eyes that really stand out in their blue-gray, flowing coats. They have full, plumed tails; ruffs around their neck; and even hair tufts between their toes. Nebelungs like their surroundings to be quiet, and so they aren't the best cats for families with young, loud children. But they become deeply attached to those they love, usually focusing their attention on one person, and will often catch a ride on his or her shoulder. Nebelungs are happy to be home alone and rarely become destructive when left to their own devices, making them a good choice for busy owners.

CAT STATS

FROM: United States
SIZE: 6–11 pounds (2.5–5 kg)
COAT: Blue
GROOMING:
CATTITUDE: Shy and gentle

NORWEGIAN FOREST CAT

With its tufted ears, plumed tail, and massive size, the Norwegian forest cat—known as the "skogkatt" in its home country—looks like a character from a folktale. Indeed—it's been featured in legends from its homeland for centuries. In Norse mythology, the Norwegian forest cat impressed the god Thor and pulled the goddess Freya's chariot. One legend even says this breed is a cross between a cat and a dog.

Fans of the breed love these cats for their large stature, flowing coat, and friendly personality. But for centuries, they were beloved mostly for their rodent-catching prowess on Norwegian farms. Before that, they were wild cats that most likely came from short-haired cats that made their way to Norway in prehistoric times.

The harsh, cold weather of their new homeland made these cats tough: Over thousands of years of evolution, they developed traits that helped them survive the wind and snow. The Norwegian forest cat's coat is both warm and water-repellent: It has a woolly undercoat that holds in heat, topped off with silky guard hairs that keep the moisture out. These cats shed their coats in summer, and, except for their fluffy tails, some even look short-haired in the warm season. But as winter approaches, they develop a full ruff—the fur around the neck—in the front and thick fur that covers their hind legs.

LONG, PLUMED TAIL

CAT STATS

FROM: Norway

SIZE: 7–20 pounds (3–9 kg)

COAT: Most solid colors, shades, and patterns

GROOMING:

CATTITUDE: Calm and friendly

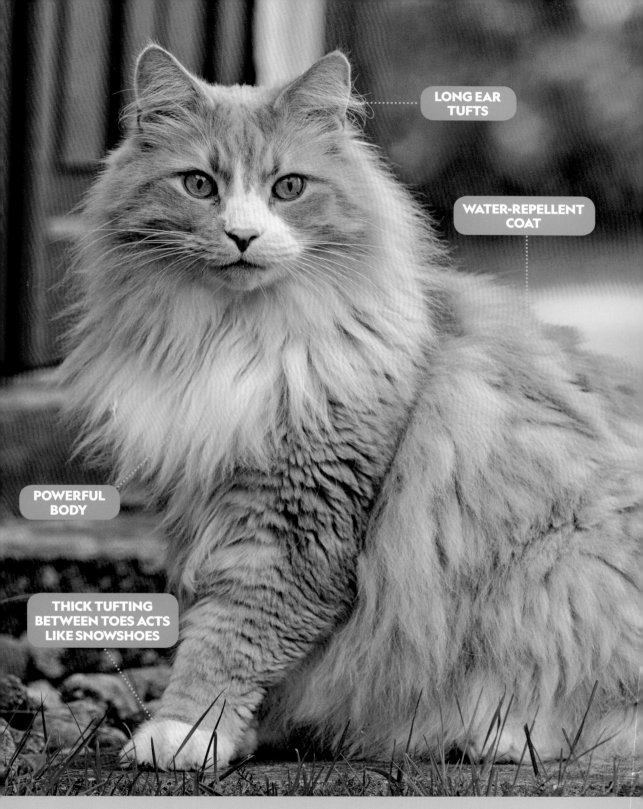

LONG EAR TUFTS

WATER-REPELLENT COAT

POWERFUL BODY

THICK TUFTING BETWEEN TOES ACTS LIKE SNOWSHOES

These kitties are adapted to a cold climate.

Norwegian forest cats have many other features that make them different from most breeds. They have long, wispy hairs tufting their ears, which help keep out wind and snow. They have large, round paws with lots of hair between the toes, which gives the cat natural snowshoes. Their hind legs are longer than their front legs, which helps them climb trees. And, since the forces of nature designed these cats, their coat thickness differs depending on their color: Darker-colored cats have slightly less fur, because their coats are better at soaking up heat from the sun than those of lighter-colored cats.

Despite their wild origins, Norwegian forest cats are sweet, friendly, and happy to make their home inside with a human family. The thousands of years they spent surviving in the forest made them sharp and intelligent, and many love to hone their hunting skills by stalking, pouncing on, and fighting toys. But, most of the time, these are calm cats that tend to get along well with other cats, dogs, kids, and visitors. Many aren't lap cats (and maybe that's a good thing, since they can be as large as 20 pounds [9 kg]). But that doesn't mean they don't like attention. They love to be pet and will often beg for a chin scratch or belly rub until their favorite human gives in.

Norwegian forest cats are **NICKNAMED "WEGIES"** (pronounced wee-gees).

ORIENTAL
LONGHAIR

Referred to by cat lovers as the "rainbow cat" or "a Siamese in designer genes," Orientals come in an almost infinite number of color and pattern combinations. These cats have all the physical characteristics of the Siamese (p. 138) with a lithe, elegant body, but it's their range of colors that sets them apart.

Orientals come in both a short-haired (p. 114) and long-haired version. Long-haired Orientals were originally called British Angoras. They were developed in the United Kingdom in the 1960s to re-create the Angora cats that were the favorite pet of Victorians until the Persians took over.

Their name was changed when people began to confuse them with the Turkish Angora (p. 248). But Orientals can trace their ancestry back much further than the 1960s—centuries, in fact. The breed is mentioned in texts dating back to the 1800s.

The word that comes to mind when looking at an Oriental is "long"—these cats have long legs, long bodies, long necks, and long, tapering tails. They also have the wedge-shaped head characteristic of Siamese cats, topped off with wide ears and almond-shaped green eyes. Their coats are fine and silky with no undercoat and require grooming only about two or three times a week.

These cats are curious and playful. They're known in the cat world for their antics, like keeping you company when you brush your teeth and helping you inspect the refrigerator when you're looking for a snack. Left alone, Orientals tend to get lonely, but given attention, they thrive.

🐾 CAT STATS

FROM: United Kingdom
SIZE: 6–11 pounds (2.5–5 kg)
COAT: Many colors and patterns
GROOMING:
CATTITUDE: Playful and loyal

WEDGE-SHAPED HEAD

TAPERING TAIL

LONG NOSE

LONG, ANGULAR BODY

Orientals are **VOCAL CATS** that will **GREET YOU AT THE DOOR** when you get home.

SLENDER LEGS

SMALL PAWS

CAT SHOWS

In dog shows, canines of all shapes and sizes race through obstacle courses and jog in sedate circles with their human handlers by their side. But what exactly happens at a *cat* show? Most people aren't familiar with these fur-filled events. But if you're a die-hard cat lover, cat shows are the best way for you to show off your prized kitties and meet other feline fanciers.

THE FIRST CAT SHOW

The world's first major cat show was held at the Crystal Palace in London in July 1871. Many historians think this fur festival was the brainchild of a man named Harrison Weir. Nicknamed the "Father of Cat Fancy," Weir went on to found the United Kingdom's National Cat Club and was the first to say that cats of an official breed had to have specific traits. He also wrote the first pedigree cat book, called *Our Cats and All About Them.*

The Crystal Palace show was an exhibition meant to show off exotic cat breeds. Around 200 fancy felines were on display for a fascinated public: Reports show that around 200,000 people visited the show. These guests likely had only ever seen mixed-breed barn cats and street cats, so they were probably amazed to view Siamese (p. 138), Manx (p. 104), Persian (p. 220), and British shorthair (p. 50) cats. Wealthy people from royal families sent their pets to be showcased, but rumors say that to fill the cages, workmen brought their own mousers (cats that catch mice) and also captured strays in the palace's cellars.

CAT CHAMPIONS OF TODAY

Weir judged the first cat show, using a set of guidelines he had written called the "Standards of Excellence." The cats on display were sorted into categories based on their traits, such as their size, body type, and coat color and length. Then they were judged based on Weir's set of standards. Many years and lots of cat shows later, these "breed standards" have been refined, but they're still how cats are judged today.

Cat shows are put on by different cat-loving organizations, like the Cat Fanciers' Association in the United States, the Governing Council of the Cat Fancy in the United Kingdom, and the International Cat Association. Each organization uses a different set of breed standards to judge the cats on how they look and act.

COMPETITION BASICS

On show day, owners wait for their turn, then bring their cat to a set of cages in the judge's ring. Judges take the cats out one by one, inspect them, and give them a rating. At the Cat Fanciers' Association shows, for example, cats can compete in four classes: the Kitten class, for cats between four and eight months old; the Championship competition, for registered cats (those that have been officially accepted into one of the breed organizations) older than eight months; the Premiership class, for registered cats older than eight months that have been spayed or neutered, and Household Pet, a class for unregistered cats older than eight months.

Do you think your cat could be a Grand Champion? If your kitty is calm and doesn't mind being handled, he or she might be the purr-fect show candidate. Check out the different cat fancy organizations to learn about competitions in your area, and show off your feline friend to the world.

ROUNDED
HEAD

BIG
ROUND
EYES

VERY
SHORT
MUZZLE

LONG, THICK,
FLUFFY COAT

THICK LEGS

PERSIAN

Sometimes called the original longhair, the Persian is perhaps the most famous cat breed in the world. By the time cat shows were becoming popular in the late 19th century, the Persian was already established as a favorite cat in the United States and the United Kingdom. Its luxurious coat is a lot of work to care for, but lovers of the breed say their cats' doll-like faces and sweet temperaments make up for all that brushing.

Despite this cat's name, no one can say for sure if its ancestors actually did come from Persia (now called Iran). This breed is so old that its origins are shrouded in mystery. Some stories say Persians hailed from the Middle East with returning Crusaders. Others say they traveled from their homeland in the wicker baskets of spice traders who sold them to European nobles fond of collecting unusual animals.

History does tell us that, in 1626, an Italian explorer named Pietro della Valle journeyed to Persia and India and brought back some cats with lots of long, fluffy hair. These cats became all the rage, and, 100 years later, another explorer from France brought back similar longhairs from Turkey. The two breeds were crossed, creating a petite white cat with a long nose and long tail. These cats crossed with local cats, and, in the 18th century, paintings began to show what look like modern-day Persians adorning the laps of elegant ladies.

Generations of breeding have created more than 100 Persian colors and patterns. There are so many colors, in fact, that the Cat Fanciers' Association divides them into several categories for showing, including solid, chinchilla, silver tabby, and tabby tricolor.

🐾 CAT STATS

FROM: United Kingdom

SIZE: 8–15 pounds (3.5–7 kg)

COAT: A wide range of colors, shades, and patterns

GROOMING:

CATTITUDE: Gentle and sweet

With their round heads and large eyes, Persian cats look like kittens all their lives. They have round bodies, small round ears, and shortened snub noses. Their features give them an innocent "Who, me?" expression that centuries of cat lovers have fallen for. Fortunately, the Persian loves humans right back.

This is a gentle cat with a trusting personality. Persians love to cuddle and prefer to have a person around at all times to keep them company. Their short legs and heavy body mean that this isn't a feline that will be climbing the curtains and getting into lots of mischief—it's entirely content to be a fluffy, purring lap cat. Persians adore attention and will follow their human around the house until they get it.

The Persian's long, fine coat must be groomed every day so mats don't form. People who compete their Persians at cat shows go to extreme lengths to keep that fluff pristine—even putting bibs on their Persians so they don't get their ruffs dirty when eating!

It's a good thing Persians **LOVE HUMAN CONTACT,** because these kitties are very **HIGH-MAINTENANCE.**

PIXIEBOB
LONGHAIR

If you've always wanted a wild bobcat for a friend, the pixiebob could be the perfect feline for you. With its stub tail, shaggy coat, and striped fur, this cat looks just like a pint-size bobcat. And that's no accident—the pixiebob was carefully bred to look like its forest-dwelling cousin. These cats are available in both a long-haired and short-haired (p. 122) version.

The breed got its beginning in 1986, when breeder Carol Ann Brewer rescued a male tabby cat of unusual stature—he stood as tall as her knees! Brewer crossed this cat with an ordinary domestic female. One of their kittens had a spotted coat and a wild look, and Brewer named her Pixie. This cat went on to lend her name to the new breed. By 1987, Brewer was on the hunt for more cats with Pixie's distinctive look. The breed was granted Championship status in 1998, making it one of the newest cat breeds out there.

Pixiebobs have stocky, muscular bodies, bobbed tails, and spotted coats, but their exotic appearance doesn't stop there. These kitties are also polydactyls—meaning they have extra toes. Whereas most cats have five toes on their front paws and four in the back, pixiebobs can have up to seven toes on each foot. There are long-haired and short-haired varieties.

Pixiebobs are highly social cats that are devoted to their families, love children, and get along well with other pets. They're known to communicate with their humans with chirps and chatters, and they never want to be left out of the action. Many pixiebob owners have trained their cat to walk on a leash so it can join in on family outings!

CAT STATS

FROM: United States
SIZE: 9–18 pounds (4–8 kg)
COAT: Brown-spotted tabby only
GROOMING:
CATTITUDE: Intelligent and loving

PEAR-SHAPED HEAD

EARS SET BACK ON SKULL

DARK FACIAL MARKINGS

Pixiebobs are sometimes called **"DOGS IN DISGUISE"** for their intelligent and loving personalities.

THICK, MUSCULAR LEGS

SHORT TAIL

BROAD HEAD

LARGE, OVAL EYES

HEAVY BODY

Ragdolls are **LAID-BACK** and choose to spend their time **SNOOZING ON THE FLOOR** instead of climbing the curtains.

RAGDOLL

If you're looking for the ultimate cuddle companion, look no further than the ragdoll. Named for its tendency to collapse happily into its owner's arms, this large, fluffy cat was practically created to snuggle.

Some say that the first ragdolls were a litter of kittens born in California that had the odd tendency of going limp and floppy when they were picked up. But the true story is that this breed was carefully created by a breeder named Ann Baker. Baker had a domestic cat with a gentle personality named Josephine. Though this cat was white, she carried a pattern on her skin, either seal mitted or tuxedo, that she passed on to her kittens. All modern ragdolls are descended from Josephine.

Once breeders of ragdolls developed the new breed, these cute kitties began to appear in the show ring. They advanced to Championship status in 2000 and haven't looked back; ragdolls are shown around the world today.

CAT STATS

FROM: United States

SIZE: 10–20 pounds (4.5–9 kg)

COAT: Most solid colors in tortie and tabby patterns; always pointed and bicolor or mitted

GROOMING:

CATTITUDE: Laid-back and gentle

LONG, PLUMED TAIL

SHORTER FUR ON LOWER LEGS

Ragdolls make loving pets.

It's not just this cat's floppy body that makes it the perfect cuddly companion: Ragdolls also have flowing coats that beg to be stroked. They're so soft they almost feel like rabbits instead of cats. Their coats come in four patterns: pointed, with Siamese-type markings; mitted, a pointed coat with white feet; bicolor, with white legs, bellies, and faces; and vans, which look like they took a dip in a pool of milk, with white bodies, point markings, and blue eyes.

Ragdolls are unusually slow-growing cats: It may take them four years to reach their adult size! Ragdoll kittens grow at all different rates—some slowly and steadily and some in spurts during which they can gain two pounds (0.9 kg) in a single month. Adult males can reach a whopping 20 pounds (9 kg). Because they love to lie on their humans, more delicate owners such as elderly people may want to opt for a lighter female ragdoll over a heavy male.

Besides their fondness for snuggling, they are generally gentle creatures that are careful with children and prefer to speak in purrs instead of loud meows. They're devoted to their people and can almost always be found purring in a lap or curled up at their owner's feet. That makes the ragdoll a great choice for families or those who live alone and are in need of some loving cat company.

SCOTTISH FOLD LONGHAIR

With its tightly folded ears, large eyes, and round head, the Scottish fold looks almost more like an owl than a cat. It may be unusual looking, but it's a real-life breed that originated roaming the farms of Scotland.

Whichever of the fold's traits you like, there's the perfect variety for you. Scottish folds can be long-haired or short-haired (p. 128), and even though they're known for their folded ears, some also have standard ears (p. 132 and p. 232).

Cats with folded ears first appeared in Scotland in 1961, in the form of a copper-eyed white female named Susie. Susie was discovered by a shepherd named William Ross, who noticed her in a new litter belonging to his farming neighbors. Ross and his wife wanted a folded-eared cat of their own, so they asked for one of Susie's kittens. In 1968, a white copper-eyed clone of her mother, a kitten named Snooks, joined the Ross family. A few careful crossings later, and the Scottish fold was born. The breed was eventually exported to America where further crosses were made with American and British shorthairs.

These cats are playful, friendly companions who thrive on affection from their owners. They don't do well with rough handling, so they might not be the best choice for energetic children. But given the right treatment, they'll bond with every member of the family. That includes other cats—although sometimes, would-be feline friends take a while to adjust to the Scottish fold's appearance. That's because folded ears are usually a cat's way of communicating anger—so they can take a little getting used to.

Scottish folds have medium-size, padded bodies, thick ruffs around their necks, and long, plumed tails. With fluffy fur covering their plump, round bodies, long-haired folds look even more like cartoon cats than their short-haired cousins.

CAT STATS

FROM: United States and United Kingdom

SIZE: 6–13 pounds (2.5–6 kg)

COAT: Most solid colors and shades; most tabby, tortie, and colorpoint patterns

GROOMING:

CATTITUDE: Gentle and friendly

SMALL, FOLDED EARS

ROUND EYES

ROUND HEAD

Most Scottish folds are **QUIET CATS.**

LONG COAT

LONG, PLUMED TAIL

STRAIGHT EARS

ROUND HEAD

LARGE EYES

Every Scottish fold and Scottish straight can trace its ancestry back to a **BARN CAT NAMED SUSIE.**

THICK COAT

SCOTTISH STRAIGHT LONGHAIR

With its normal, upright ears, you'd never guess the origins of the Scottish straight— but this cat has the same genes as its folded-eared cousin, the Scottish fold (p. 230). The gene that causes the fold's bent-over ears is a spontaneous mutation that comes from a type of gene classified as an incomplete dominant—it results in half of the litter having folded ears and half having straight ears.

All Scottish kittens are born with straight ears. It's only after they're about three weeks old that the ears of the folds cats begin to bend. Cats whose ears remain straight are classified as Scottish straights.

Since the first Scottish was discovered, in 1961, these cats have developed into a family breed beloved for their sweet personalities and unusual appearances. The cats in the Scottish family (fold and straight, in long-haired and short-haired coats) have an overall round appearance. Their bodies are round and chubby, their heads are round with big round eyes, and even their paws are round.

Cats in the Scottish family are still rare as household pets. But they're becoming increasingly popular, in part for their loyal, loving natures. They are easygoing felines that adjust well to many types of families and are quietly affectionate companions who are glad to sit and purr happily in their favorite person's lap.

CAT STATS

FROM: United States and United Kingdom

SIZE: 6–13 pounds (2.5–6 kg)

COAT: Most solid colors and shades; most tabby, tortie, and colorpoint patterns

GROOMING:

CATTITUDE: Loyal and loving

PLUMED TAIL

CATS IN JAPAN

It could be said that there's no place in the world where cats are more beloved than in Japan. From the waving kitty sculptures that adorn nearly every restaurant to the cat cafés where visitors can spend a free hour making new furry friends, it's fair to say that the country is cat-obsessed. And history shows that Japan's dedication to the feline is nothing new.

CATS CONQUER THE COUNTRY

Cats probably arrived in Japan about 1,000 years ago on ships from China. These sailor cats were mousers, but the Japanese saw something special in these new whiskered creatures from across the sea. Cats proved adept at keeping rodents from snacking on the parchment used to record important religious documents, and they quickly became temple protectors.

Cats were so rare and special back then that, by the 10th century B.C., only the elite could afford to own them. Art from the time shows their esteemed status: Cats were often depicted living indoors and parading around on leashes. A cat even played a starring role in a popular story of the time called *The Tale of Genji*, in which a kitty sets a chain of events into action when it knocks over a folding screen.

But cats received a blow to their status in 1602. Japan's silk industry was in danger of collapsing as a result of rats and mice preying on the silkworms. The government decreed that all pet cats had to be set free to battle the enemy rodents. All those free cats resulted in a lot of kittens, and cats were no longer rare. But they were still special.

CATS IN ART AND LEGEND

During the Edo period, which lasted from 1603 to 1868, Japan introduced a new type of art called *ukiyo-e*. In the days before the internet and TV, *ukiyo-e* was a major form of entertainment. It was made by carving an image in to a piece of wood, applying paint, and then stamping it onto paper. Unlike earlier art, it could be mass-produced, and suddenly art was available to everyone. And cats were one of the most popular subjects.

Cats were a favorite character in Japanese folklore, too. One story tells of a wealthy man who took shelter under a tree during a rainstorm. While huddled against the downpour, he spotted a cat doing something strange—it appeared to be beckoning to him. After the bewildered man followed the feline inside a nearby temple, the tree he had been standing under was struck by lightning. Because the cat had saved his life, the man gratefully donated to the temple, and when he passed away, the cat was honored with a statue. Some say this was the origin of the Japanese "lucky cat" called Maneki Neko. Figurines of this white cat with the raised paw adorn shops and restaurants all over Japan. Legend says that if the cat's right paw is raised, it brings good luck, and if its left paw is raised, it welcomes customers.

FAMOUS FELINES OF TODAY

Visit Japan today and you'll see cats everywhere. Of course there's Hello Kitty, the iconic white cat with the pink bow who started out in the 1950s as the spokescat for a Japanese company that sold gifts. Today, she can be seen on more than 20,000 official products, from shoes to guitars to airplanes. There's even a Hello Kitty hospital in Taiwan, where nurses wear uniforms picturing the popular feline (pictured, left).

Cats star in Japan's animated cartoons and graphic novels and gather millions of comments in internet videos. Real-life cats are popular, too: Besides cat cafés, where cat lovers enjoy a cup of coffee or tea along with a kitty snuggle, there's Aoshima, a popular vacation destination nicknamed "Cat Island." There, felines outnumber humans six to one. No one knows what new kitty trend will crop up next, but one thing is for sure: Japan is a claw-some place to be if you're a cat lover.

SELKIRK REX
LONGHAIR

Known for its unusual curly coat, the Selkirk rex comes in both short-haired (p. 136) and long-haired varieties, but long-haired Selkirks are the ones that really show off that remarkable fur.

The Selkirk rex got its start when a curly-coated kitten was discovered in a litter of otherwise normal-coated kittens in an animal rescue center in Montana. Crossings with Persians (p. 220) went on to create the modern Selkirk rex longhair.

Every hair on a Selkirk rex's body is curly, right down to the whiskers. As they grow, Selkirk kittens can go back and forth from looking extra-curly to an almost-straight coat. But someone interested in an especially curly Selkirk should choose the curliest kitten in the litter, as those are most likely to keep their curl into adulthood. Their curl is most dramatic on their flanks, belly, and around the neck. Though this cat might look like a lot of maintenance, owners are actually advised not to brush their cats too much, as that can straighten their ringlets.

The Selkirk rex's unique coat may have been what caught the eye of cat fanciers at first, but this cat's pleasant personality is what makes it a favorite household pet. Selkirk rexes are sweet-tempered and gentle. They're known as teddy bears, and they love a cuddle so much that they'll often beg their owners for attention—or jump in a free lap whenever they spot one.

CAT STATS

FROM: United States
SIZE: 8–11 pounds (3.5–5 kg)
COAT: All colors, shades, and patterns
GROOMING:
CATTITUDE: Sweet and cuddly

CURLY COAT

LARGE, ROUND EYES

Selkirk rex's kinked whiskers **ARE BRITTLE** and can sometimes **BREAK OFF.**

SHORT, SQUARE MUZZLE

LONGER CURLS AROUND RUFF

HEAVY BODY

SIBERIAN

The Siberian, Russia's national cat, got its beginning in the forests of its native land. Today this plush, affectionate clown is more at home in *your* home; these cats love people and are beloved in turn for their big personalities.

Siberians are an ancient breed that first appeared in recorded history around the year A.D. 1,000. They were the prized pest exterminators of Russian farmers and tradespeople, who would boast and brag to each other about whose kitty had the thickest and most luxurious coat. Many Russians kept pet cats, and Siberians were the most popular breed. They were even cast as characters in Russian fairy tales, often as magical beings who protected children and had the ability to open doorways to otherworldly lands.

Though they were known to exist in Russia through the Middle Ages, very few Siberians made their way outside their home country's borders back then. However, they did make their way into cat shows: The Siberian was one of the three long-haired cats represented at the world's first cat show in 1871. When Russia came under Soviet rule from 1917 to 1927, the keeping of pet cats was discouraged due to housing and food shortages, and it seemed like the Siberian could be lost forever. But lovers of the breed came to its rescue, breeding the Siberians that were left to rebuild their numbers, and by the late 1980s, they had officially put the Siberian on the map.

TRIPLE-LAYERED COAT

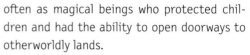

CAT STATS

FROM: Russia
SIZE: 10–20 pounds (4.5–9 kg)
COAT: All colors and patterns
GROOMING: 🐾🐾🐾🐾🐾
CATTITUDE: Friendly and loyal

SHORT, ROUNDED MUZZLE

FULL, EXTRA-FLUFFY TAIL

THICK RUFF AROUND NECK

LARGE, ROUND, TUFTED PAWS

Some people with cat allergies are **NOT ALLERGIC** to Siberians.

 Siberians have a regal look.

Siberians are medium-to-large cats with heavy limbs, broad bodies, and big paws. They have very dense, water-resistant, triple-layered coats that grow into thick ruffs around their necks and long, fluffy tails. Because their coats mat easily, experts advise grooming them daily to remove tangles.

Siberians might look like an allergy-sufferer's nightmare, but there is some evidence that these cats may actually be a great choice for people who are allergic to cats. Though it hasn't been scientifically proven, many people who suffer cat allergies seem to be able to cuddle Siberians with no sniffling or sneezing. Some people think that this is due to a genetic mutation that gives Siberians lower-than-normal levels of a certain enzyme in their saliva. Though many people believe they are allergic to cat *fur*, the real culprit is often this enzyme, which gets on a cat's fur when it licks itself. Allergy sufferers interested in Siberians should visit a breeder (some will even send a fur sample in the mail) to see if they are in the lucky group of allergy sufferers who have no trouble with Siberians.

The Siberian's plush coat may be what gets this cat noticed, but Siberians have stuck around for so long as favorite pets because of their friendly, loyal personalities. Many Siberians will meet their owners of the door and tell their humans all about their day in a series of trills and chirps. If you enjoy your alone time, this is probably not the cat for you; Siberians will watch TV with you, insist on "helping" you while you work on the computer or read a book, and will curl up by your side at night, purring.

CAT HEROES

We've all heard tales of dogs leaping into freezing lakes to save a struggling swimmer or bravely bolting into burning buildings to rescue a frightened child. But cats can be heroes, too. These fearless felines faced down battles, fires, and medical emergencies—all to help another creature in need. And all they wanted in return was a few chin scratches.

SIMON THE SHIP SAVIOR

When a 17-year-old British sailor smuggled a cat named Simon onto the H.M.S. *Amethyst* in 1948, the crew had no idea the little black-and-white kitty would soon save their lives. The first few months onboard were smooth sailing, and Simon proved himself an expert mouser who could take care of any hungry rats onboard. But when the ship ran into an ambush while sailing up China's Yangtze River, Simon's pest patrol became a life-or-death matter. Enemy fire disabled the ship, and the crew was held captive on the wounded vessel. With no ability to restock their rations, the sailors couldn't afford to lose an ounce of food to rats. Though Simon had been injured in the battle, he went right to work protecting the food stores. Without his fighting spirit, the soldiers would have starved. When the ship returned safely to shore, the brave cat was awarded the PDSA Dickin Medal for outstanding animal bravery under enemy fire.

PUDDITAT THE SEEING-EYE KITTY

When a gray-and-white house cat showed up on Judy Godfrey-Brown's doorstep in Anglesey, Wales, she couldn't turn him away. The animal lover already had a houseful of pets. So Pudditat came right in—and made a beeline for Godfrey-Brown's dog. The chocolate Labrador mix named Terfel had been abused as a pup, and he was blind and partially deaf. He was too fearful to go outside and rarely left his bed. But that all changed when Pudditat joined the family. Though he had no interest in the other pets, the cat formed a bond with the disabled dog, rarely leaving Terfel's side and running his face against the dog's neck and legs. Before long, Pudditat was coaxing the timid pup to leave his bed and take walks around the yard. Totally trusting Pudditat, Terfel would follow closely behind his guide cat. The bond between the two creatures never faltered, and the pair remained close until the dog passed away from old age—after countless walks with his feline friend.

MONTY THE ALARM CAT

Patricia Peter was disappointed when she drove to her local humane society to pick out a new kitten and found that they'd all been adopted already. But when an adult orange tabby snuggled up to her, Peter knew she couldn't leave without him. She named the cat Monty and brought him home to Camrose, Alberta, Canada. Monty became Peter's devoted companion, sleeping at her feet and greeting her at the door when she came home from work. So when he bit her finger one night while she was sleeping, Peter was surprised—and annoyed. That is, until she realized she was sweating, dizzy, and shaking. Newly diagnosed with diabetes, Peter was suffering from diabetic shock. She took her medication right away—without it, she could have slipped into a diabetic coma. In the years since, Monty has alerted Peter when her blood sugar dropped—and kept her alive—dozens of times.

NUDGE THE FELINE FIRE LOOKOUT

Nudge the Maine coon got her name for her habit of affectionately head-butting her owner, Nic Pascal, of Jamesville, New York, U.S.A. Dumped in the woods near his house by a previous owner, Nudge was fearful at first, but she soon warmed up to her new family. She spent her days cozied up indoors with her human buddies, with trips outside to the hunt moles, mice, and chipmunks who lived in the forest. Then came the morning of April 9, 2010. Pascal woke up to the usually silent Nudge jumping on his chest and caterwauling into his ear. He pushed her off, but she leapt on again—this time with her claws out. Annoyed, Pascal got up and walked into the hall—to discover black smoke billowing out of his garage. The house was on fire! Pascal dialed 911, and firefighters were able to save his house with minimal damage—all thanks to the brave kitty who thanked Pascal for rescuing her by rescuing him in return.

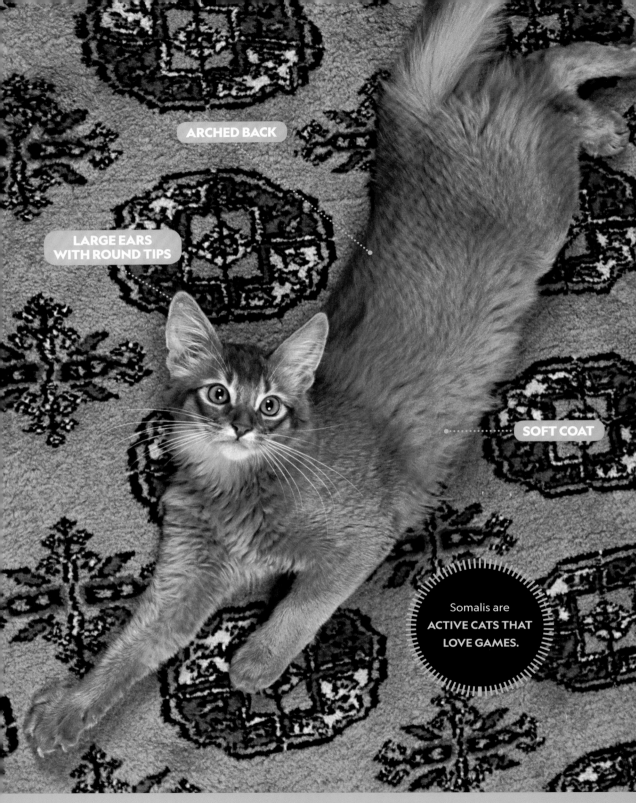

ARCHED BACK

LARGE EARS
WITH ROUND TIPS

SOFT COAT

Somalis are
**ACTIVE CATS THAT
LOVE GAMES.**

SOMALI

When a genetic mutation occurred by chance in Abyssinian cats (p. 28), resulting in long-haired kittens, breeders weren't interested at first. But some found these graceful cats with the full coats lovely to look at. Breeders caught on, and these kitties eventually became their own breed: the Somali. They were officially recognized by the Cat Fanciers' Association in 1979.

When many people first meet a Somali, they remark that it looks like a fox. That's because many have reddish coats that are ticked with brown, giving them a glowing appearance. Like foxes, they also have large ears and exceptionally long, bushy tails. It can take up to 18 months for a young Somali's adult coat color to develop. Though they have thick coats, most don't tangle easily, and Somali owners can get away with combing their cats just two to three times a week.

Somalis are curious, alert creatures with lots of energy to play. They're not exactly lap cats, preferring to spend their time on the move. They love to open cupboards and doors, goad you into a game of hide-and-seek, and romp with the dog; Somalis easily make friends. All this activity might sound exhausting, but Somalis are sweet creatures who love to please, and they put their energy toward entertaining their owners.

DARK MARKINGS ON FACE

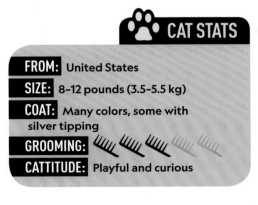

CAT STATS

FROM: United States
SIZE: 8–12 pounds (3.5–5.5 kg)
COAT: Many colors, some with silver tipping
GROOMING:
CATTITUDE: Playful and curious

LONG, BUSHY TAIL

TIFFANIE

It was a happy accident when a male Persian chinchilla was crossed with a lilac female Burmese, because the result was the Asian breed of cats—a group that includes the cuddly Tiffanie. People found the kittens from that first litter of Tiffanies so beautiful that they were all snapped up fast—and it was the beginning of a new breed.

Tiffanie cats get their striking silver coloring and tipped markings from the chinchilla, a type of Persian (p. 220), but their friendly, curious personalities come from the Burmese (p. 58). Crosses between chinchillas and Burmese result in both short-haired and long-haired kittens. The short-haired kittens are called Burmillas (p. 60), and the long-haired ones are Tiffanies. The breed is currently recognized by a British organization called the Governing Council of the Cat Fancy but not yet by American or international organizations.

Tiffanies have medium-length, silky coats with a thick ruff around the neck; a long, plumed tail; and yellow-green eyes that are set wide apart in their faces. If you're looking for a cuddly companion, the Tiffanie might be the kitty for you. These cats crave attention and need to feel like part of the family. If they're left solo too often, Tiffanies will get lonely, so they're best for owners who are usually home. Tiffanie owners say their cats are highly sensitive to their feelings, making them ideal pets for someone who is looking for a close relationship that will last a lifetime.

CAT STATS

FROM: United States

SIZE: 8–14 pounds (3.5–6.5 kg)

COAT: All solid and shaded colors in tabby and tortie patterns

GROOMING:

CATTITUDE: Sensitive and loving

LONG TAIL

OVAL PAWS

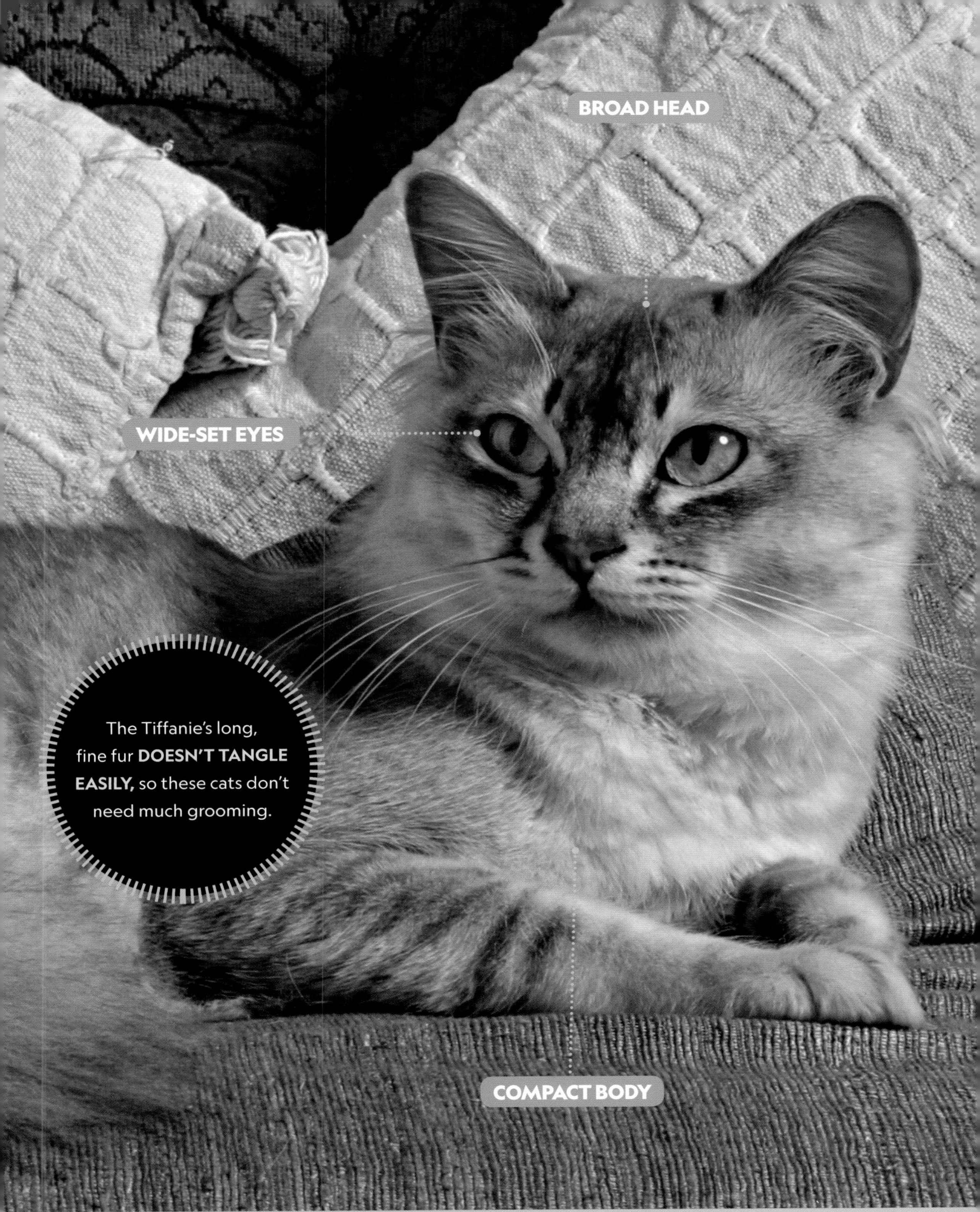

BROAD HEAD

WIDE-SET EYES

The Tiffanie's long, fine fur **DOESN'T TANGLE EASILY,** so these cats don't need much grooming.

COMPACT BODY

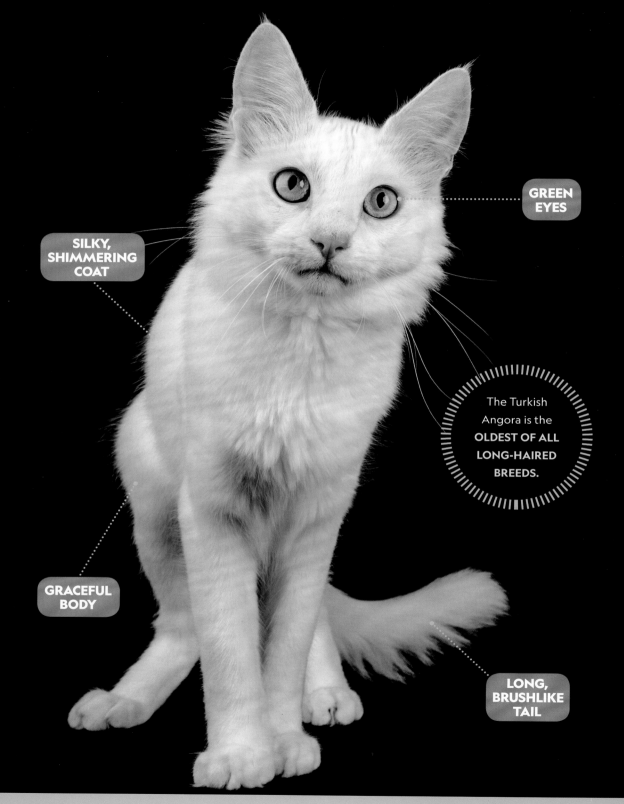

GREEN
EYES

SILKY,
SHIMMERING
COAT

The Turkish
Angora is the
**OLDEST OF ALL
LONG-HAIRED
BREEDS.**

GRACEFUL
BODY

LONG,
BRUSHLIKE
TAIL

TURKISH ANGORA

If your dream pet is a kitty with a coat as soft as a rabbit's, you might have met your perfect match. The Turkish Angora's coat is so silky it shines in the light. And it has the perfect personality for petting: Loyal and loving, it's a cat that bonds tightly to its family.

Records of this cat with the shiny coat date back to the 16th century, but experts think it probably originated several centuries before that. It may be native to Turkey, or it may have been introduced there in the 12th century by the Tartars, an ancient tribal people who hailed from the Mongolian plateau. When the Turkish Angora first arrived in Europe during the Renaissance, it was crossed with the Persian. By World War II, the two breeds had merged so much that the Turkish Angora had almost become extinct. Turkish authorities rounded up all the cats of their national breed they could find and began a breeding program to bring them back from the brink.

Graceful and athletic, Turkish Angoras love nothing more than chasing a mouse—whether a real one or a toy version—across the room. This is one breed that hasn't lost touch with its wild roots. Turkish Angoras' exceptional intelligence makes these cats excellent hunters, but stalking and pouncing aren't their only interest: They are loyal pets that are totally devoted to their owners.

LARGE, TUFTED EARS

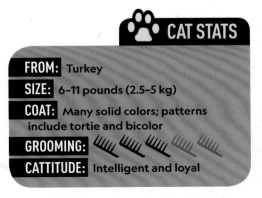

CAT STATS

FROM: Turkey

SIZE: 6–11 pounds (2.5–5 kg)

COAT: Many solid colors; patterns include tortie and bicolor

GROOMING:

CATTITUDE: Intelligent and loyal

TURKISH VAN

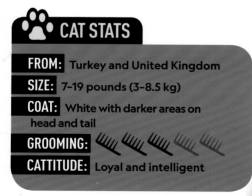

If one person in your family wants a cat, and another is set on a dog, the Turkish Van might be the ideal compromise. This elegant white cat with the inquisitive eyes has many characteristics people normally associate with canines: It's a steadfast friend to its human family and loves to play fetch. Many even enjoy a dip in the pool.

The Turkish Van hails from the Middle East or Central and Southwest Asia, where it has been a native cat for a very long time. Carvings on jewelry dated to between 1600 and 1200 B.C. depict white-haired cats with dark tails. Later, a legion of the Roman army used a cat fitting the same description on its armor and battle flags. Two thousand years after that, two photographers from England were traveling around Turkey when they received a pair of these cats as gifts. Back in England, those cats became the foundation breeding pair of the modern breed. Today, the Turkish Van is an official breed recognized around the world—especially in Turkey, where it is considered a national treasure.

DARK MARKINGS ON HEAD AND TAIL

CAT STATS

FROM: Turkey and United Kingdom

SIZE: 7–19 pounds (3–8.5 kg)

COAT: White with darker areas on head and tail

GROOMING:

CATTITUDE: Loyal and intelligent

LONG, BRUSHLIKE TAIL

LARGE EYES, OFTEN ODD-COLORED

MUSCULAR BODY

SOFT, WATER-RESISTANT COAT

Turkish Vans are famous for their **LOVE OF WATER.**

Turkish Vans are also called Vans or Vancats. ("Van" is a name given to many towns in Turkey.) They are known for their semi-long, extremely soft fur and extra-long, feathered tail. These cats come in a "van" pattern, an all-white coat with darker markings on the head and tail and sometimes on the back. The dark patches can be a variety of colors including red, black, brown tabby, or patched tabby. Vans have long, plush tails that the cats often flick back and forth to express their happiness. And they have striking eyes, which come in amber, bright blue, or odd-colored, with one blue and one amber. The gene that results in odd-colored eyes is also responsible for white spots on the coat, so the two traits always occur together.

Under all that fluff is a strong, muscular body, and a brain of exceptional intelligence. Most Vans love nothing more than a game of fetch, and your arm will probably tire of throwing your Van's favorite toy long before your cat is worn out. Vans are also excellent at solving problems. Sometimes, this can get them into trouble, like when they figure out how to climb into an off-limits cabinet! But most Van owners like these cats' impish side and consider them big clowns who provide endless entertainment.

Vans are sometimes nicknamed "swimming cats" because of their most unusual attribute: a love of water. Experts think that this cat may have originated in the Lake Van region of Turkey, where they were many inviting mountain streams to cool off in during the hot Turkish summers. Not all Vans like to swim, but some will indeed take a dip if there's a pool or pond available. And nearly all Vans find running water irresistible—so if you get a Van of your own, don't be surprised if your new buddy joins you in the shower!

OWNING
A CAT

Has scanning these pages of fantastic felines made you want a kitty to call your own? There's a reason people have been making cats part of their families for thousands of years. Pet cats are adorable balls of fur that snooze in the sunshine, gracefully streak through the living room, and pounce on a toy for the amusement of everyone watching. They are cuddle buddies that will warm your lap—and your heart.

Having a cat for a pet means a lifetime of friendship, but it's also a big responsibility. Read on to get the 411 on all aspects of cat ownership, from how to choose your new best friend to how to keep your cat healthy and happy for years to come. Your new kitty buddy is sure to appreciate that you did your homework.

HOW TO CHOOSE
THE RIGHT CAT
FOR YOU

So you're ready to be a cat owner. It's time for the fun part: deciding which cat to make your forever friend. The world of cat breeds is big: Do you want a big fur ball like a Maine coon? A fancy feline like a Persian? An athletic kitty like an ocicat? Or might a mixed breed be the best choice? Use this cool chart to help you narrow down your search and make your decision. No matter what, you're bound to end up with a best buddy for life.

START

I love the look of long-haired cats.

I'm looking for a playmate.

I want a fancy feline.

I want a cat with a colorful coat.

I want a cat that shows its wild side.

Brushing doesn't bother me.

Let's keep the grooming minimal.

BRITISH LONGHAIR
This teddy bear in cat's clothing comes in all colors, shades, and patterns (p. 180).

PIXIEBOB LONGHAIR
This tabby looks like a teeny tiny bobcat (p. 224).

PERSIAN
That fancy fur takes some upkeep, but this kitty's sweet temperament is worth it (p. 220).

TIFFANIE
This cross between a chinchilla and a Burmese has a long coat, but it doesn't tangle easily (p. 246).

NO PEDIGREE? NO PROBLEM.

If you have your heart set on a ragdoll, toyger, or Devon rex, you may have to get a cat from a breeder. But if it's the inside that counts for you, consider a mixed-breed cat. Though they don't have ancestors that won in the show ring, they still make wonderful pets. And adopting a mixed-breed domestic cat means you can give a home to a kitty in need. See more about adopting on page 260.

Short hair sounds more my speed.

I'd love a lap cat.

Nothing sounds cooler than a kitty that does tricks.

Someone in my house has allergies.

I want something exotic.

Personality is my priority.

SIBERIAN
Many allergy sufferers are able to tolerate these cuddly kitties, which seem to produce less of the sneeze-causing molecule (p. 238).

SCOTTISH FOLD
Bonus: These champion snugglers look like stuffed animals (p. 128).

BENGAL
This cross between an Asian leopard cat and a domestic cat looks like it would be right at home in the jungle (p. 44).

SIAMESE
These talkative, graceful cats will keep you company all day long (p. 138).

PREPARING FOR A
FELINE FRIEND

With their tiny meows and unsteady way of walking, kittens are irresistible. But before you scoop one up, consider that choosing a cat is a big decision and a long commitment.

ARE YOU READY?

Read through the following questions to help decide if you're prepared to take on a feline family member. **IF YOU SAY "YES" TO ALL OF THEM, YOU'RE PREPARED FOR CAT OWNERSHIP!**

ENDURANCE

Are you willing to care for a cat for as long as it lives— 15 years or more?

CLEANLINESS

Can you commit to feeding your cat every day and keeping the litter box clean?

COMPANIONSHIP

Can you commit to not leaving your cat alone for long periods? Some cats are more independent than others, but if the house is frequently empty for long periods, a fish might be a better pet.

ATTENTION

All cats need interaction and activity. Can you give your cat attention every day?

FINANCES

Pets are expensive. Can your family put aside funds for the vet visits, food, toys, litter box supplies, and grooming tools?

GROOMING

Will you groom a cat regularly? Even shorthairs need occasional brushing.

CLAWING

Are you (and your parents) OK with the possibility of your furniture getting clawed? Scratching is a natural behavior, and, unfortunately, many cats use the sofa. While you can encourage them to use their claws on scratching posts instead, you can never be sure your furniture will be 100 percent safe.

CAT

BREEDER VS. RESCUE

Congratulations! You're ready to take on a new feline friend. You've got lots of cuddles in your future. But first you have to decide: Is it best for you to purchase a cat from a breeder or adopt one from a shelter or rescue?

If you have your heart set on a specific breed, getting a kitten from a breeder may be the best choice. Though purebred cats can sometimes be found at shelters, you won't get the papers to confirm that a rescue is 100 percent Persian (p. 220) or Siamese (p. 138) or whichever purebred you're looking for. Sometimes, you might be able to find a specific breed through an organization that rehomes Persians, Maine coons, or whatever cat you have your heart set on. All cats are individuals, but a purebred cat's looks and behavior are more predictable than a mixed breed's. And if you're looking for one of the more exotic breeds, like the munchkin (p. 108) or Bengal (p. 44), you'll probably be able to find them only through a breeder. Some breeders cross cats carefully to ensure the healthiest kittens possible, meaning fewer veterinary problems as they get older. However, just because a cat is purebred is no guarantee that she's healthy. To increase your chances of finding a healthy cat and a reputable breeder, ask a vet for a breeder recommendation, and make sure the cat comes with a certificate of health from a vet.

There are millions of cats in shelters that need loving homes. If you don't care about having a specific breed, you might be the perfect person to save a shelter kitty. Bonus: mixed-breed cats often suffer from fewer health problems than their purebred cousins. Even if you do want a certain kind of cat, try checking a shelter for the breed you have in mind—sometimes, pedigreed cats find their way into shelters, and they need homes, too. If you're hoping to raise a cat from kittenhood, you'll be able to find a young kitty in a shelter. Just be sure to look for kittens during "kitten season," which runs from April to November. And if you'd prefer an older cat with an established personality, there are many of those waiting to be rescued, also. Many shelter cats have already been vaccinated, microchipped, and spayed or neutered, so an adoption fee is all you'll have to pay. And you'll enjoy the satisfaction of having saved a life—and deserve all the purrs you'll get!

CHOOSING
A CAT

How do you pick the perfect kitten from a litter or choose the best shelter cat from a wall of cages? Whether you choose to get a cat from a breeder or adopt one, it's best to introduce yourself to new animals slowly. Resist the urge to pick up a cat right away—instead, let your new buddy come up to you.

Spend some time with the cats and remember that just because one cat happens to be playing and another sleeping during your visit, it doesn't mean the first is active and the second is lazy. Ask the breeder or shelter worker about the cat's personality, and don't rush to decide. After all, you're not just choosing a cat—you're meeting your new best friend.

PAWS BEFORE PURCHASE

Never buy a kitten or cat over the internet. You won't know exactly where that cat came from or how she was raised. Always meet the breeder or the staff at a shelter. Talking to the people who were responsible for caring for your new friend is the best way to know how to care for her.

BRINGING KITTY
HOME

Once you've found the perfect breeder or shelter, it's time to prepare for your new feline friend to join your family. Read our tips and then check out our guide to the first days at home with your new furry buddy. Hint: It's all about taking it slow.

FIRST DAYS WITH YOUR NEW FRIEND

When you bring a new cat home, your goal is to help him feel comfortable in the unfamiliar environment as soon as possible. Everyone—especially kids—will be excited to play with the new kitty, but let your cat proceed at his own pace. With the right treatment, most cats settle into their new home quickly. Then, everyone will enjoy playtime.

Before you bring your new friend home, check your house or yard for hazards, like sharp objects. Some cats are picky eaters, so it's best to have several types of cat food on hand so you can see which one your new buddy likes best. If you got your new cat from a shelter, they'll probably give you a bag of the food they were feeding. Also, if you ask, some pet stores will give out samples that are perfect for trying out.

Plan to have your new kitty arrive on a day when the house is calm. Choose one or two rooms to restrict your cat to until he relaxes. When you get him inside the house, set his carrier inside this space and open the door so he can come out when he's ready. Make sure his litter box and food and water bowls are easy for him to see and access. (But never put a cat's litter box and feeding station next to each other.)

Now, sit back and give your cat a chance to explore. Cats are so curious that even a timid one will come out of the carrier eventually. One way to help your cat get comfortable is by playing with him using a wand toy. When a cat's hunting instincts are triggered, he becomes more confident and not as afraid. Once your cat seems calm and relaxed, you can slowly enlarge his area until he feels comfortable in the whole house. For some cats, this might take days; others will be king of their new castle in just a few hours.

MEETING THE FAMILY

If your new cat is wary of you at first, sit in the room with him and talk to him in a soft voice to get him used to your presence. Don't chase after him, and give him plenty of time to get used to you. Take it slow when introducing your new cat to people or pets. Small children may get really excited around a new cat—so show them how to stay calm, pet the kitty gently, and hold her correctly. If the cat looks stressed, let her have her space.

It may take a while for a family cat to get used to a new cat. Keep them in different areas at first, but allow them to get used to each other's scent—try switching their food bowls and bringing a blanket one cat has snoozed on to the other cat to sniff. After about a week, introduce the cats, but don't leave them alone until they seem totally calm together.

Dogs and cats often learn to become best buddies, but it doesn't always happen right away. Help them get used to each other before they meet by bringing each animals' blankets or toys to the other. This will help them learn each other's scents. When you introduce them, keep the dog on a leash, and let the cat have space to back away. Keep sessions short and don't leave the two animals alone together until you're sure they'll keep the peace.

CAT CARE

Cats are pretty self-sufficient pets. Unlike dogs, they don't need to be taken for daily walks or let out every few hours to potty. But they still require care. Feeding, grooming, socializing, and playing with your cat are the keys to keeping your pet happy. The good news is that these aren't just chores—they're a great way for you to bond with your buddy.

WHAT TO FEED YOUR CAT

The right diet is the best way to help your cat live a long and healthy life. So what to feed your feline friend?

Though most domestic cats have developed the ability to digest some plants, cats are carnivores at heart. They have to eat meat because they can't get all the nutrients they need out of vegetables and grains. And meat is the only source of a molecule called taurine that cats must have to survive. So even if you're a vegetarian yourself, your cat can't be.

Wild cats get all the protein they need from the prey they catch—plus other essential nutrients like fats, vitamins, and minerals. Because domestic cats don't hunt for their dinner, they need to eat a diet that provides all of these essentials. Commercial cat foods provide a complete diet. Look for a food that lists meat, like fish or chicken, as the first ingredient. Avoid foods that say "meat by-product" or "meal" or include a lot of grains such as corn, which cats aren't adapted to eat too much of. And make sure your kitty has fresh, clean water at all times. Cats don't tend to drink as much water as we'd like, so it's a good idea to make canned food at least a part of their daily diet.

HOW TO GROOM

Luckily, cats take care of most of the grooming work themselves. By licking their fur, they spread oils from their skin over the hair to keep it shiny and waterproofed. Tiny barbs on their tongues pull out dirt and comb out loose hair.

Even though your cat may spend a lot of her waking hours cleaning herself, she still needs your help in the grooming department. Grooming helps prevent tangles and reduces the amount of fur your cat swallows. Cats cough up most of this hair as harmless hairballs, but sometimes, fur balls can get lodged in the intestine, causing serious problems. One way to avoid this is to give them a weekly dose of a hairball remedy, which moves those hair clumps safely out. Older cats or cats with certain health conditions, like arthritis, can have a hard time grooming themselves, so it's a good idea to lend them a hand.

Start grooming your cat as early as you can to get him used to the idea. Once they're accustomed to the process, grooming becomes many cats' favorite activity. For short-haired cats, start by using a fine-toothed comb to loosen dead hair and skin, then follow up with a fine slicker brush or soft brush to remove the hair. For long-haired cats, first gently remove tangles with a wide-toothed comb, then use a slicker brush to collect loose hair. To finish, fluff up the coat with a brush or comb. And don't forget to keep your cat's nails trimmed—a task you should do about once every ten days or two weeks. Handling your cat's paws frequently from a young age will help him relax during nail-trimming time, but some cats find the experience stressful, so for them it's best to enlist the help of a grooming professional.

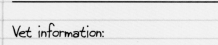

CAT SITTER'S CHECKLIST

What happens if you have to go out of town and leave your furry friend in the care of someone else? Make sure to leave detailed instructions to make sure your cat and caretaker are both happy while you're gone. Here's a checklist to help you:

Where you can be reached:
_____

Vet information:
_____

Emergency vet information:
_____

Feeding instructions:
_____

Litter box instructions:
_____

Play instructions:
_____

Grooming instructions:
_____

Medication instructions:
_____

SOCIALIZING YOUR CAT

Wild cats live alone, snoozing in hidey-holes during the day and emerging for solo hunting sessions at night. Because of their ancestry, domestic cats are also independent animals by nature. But with the right socialization, your cat can learn to live happily with people, dogs, and other cats.

The best way to socialize a cat is to start when she's a kitten. Introduce your kitten to friends, neighbors, and the vet early on. The more people she meets when she's young, the better. Keep sessions short and reward your kitten with pats and treats to teach her that new experiences are fun, not scary.

If you're adopting an adult cat, it may take him longer to get used to new people and situations. Give him time to explore unfamiliar environments and let him come up to new people and pets in his own time.

MAKING PLAYTIME FUN

In the wild, cats spend lots of time climbing trees and chasing after prey. So to stay happy and healthy, domestic cats need activity and excitement in their lives, too.

Outdoor cats get plenty of chances to run and romp, but indoor cats can get bored without stimulation, leading to behavioral problems (read more about keeping your cat indoors vs. outdoors on p. 272). Sometimes, indoor cats burn their extra energy by darting around the room, eyes wide, leaping off furniture and climbing the curtains, then running away. This is normal cat behavior—and a good source of laughs!

Toys are a great way to satisfy your cat's hunting instincts. Interactive toys like play wands allow cats and their owners to bond while blowing off steam. Cats also like toys that move, make noise, or have interesting textures. Cat trees are a great way for cats to exercise their climbing instinct and scratch something that isn't the furniture. But you don't need to spend a lot of money to keep your kitty entertained. Your cat will love a wadded-up piece of paper, a pile of tissue paper, or a paper bag from the grocery store just as much as he loves the pet store's most expensive toy.

GROWING UP
KITTEN

Is there anything cuter than a kitten? With their big round eyes, stubby tails held high, and shaky legs, they're determined to explore the world around them ... until they get sleepy and have to curl up for a catnap! Raising one of these purring bundles of fur is a lot of fun, but it comes with obligations. Here's a guide to break it all down.

1. LEARN THE AGES AND STAGES

For the first week of their lives, kittens are blind and deaf. They rely completely on their mothers to take care of them. At two weeks, their eyes open and they start to react to the world around them. By the time they're about four weeks old, they're off and running and spend a lot of their time playing and exploring. The mother begins to wean them from her milk around this age. At 8 to 12 weeks, kittens are ready to leave their litter and go live with their new families.

2. BE PREPARED

Before you bring your new kitten home, pick up all the equipment you'll need: a cat carrier, food, food and water dishes, a litter box and litter, a bed, a scratching post, a brush, and a few fun toys.

3. BRINGING HOME BABY

Decide on an area that will be your kitten's home base. Pick a quiet spot where your little fur ball will feel calm and safe, and set up her food and water dishes, litter box, and a warm, comfortable place to sleep. (Don't forget that cats don't like their food and litter box to be close together.) When you bring home your kitten, set her carrier in this space, open the door, and let her come out whenever she feels ready. Make sure to have plenty of toys to entertain her, and be sure to never play with your kitten by wiggling your fingers—that can teach her to bite.

4. FEEDING TIME

Kittens are busy growing, and they need a lot of energy to do it. That means they eat a lot—up to three times more calories than adult cats. It's best to feed them a high-quality food specially formulated for kittens. Many vets recommend "free-feeding" or leaving food out all the time so kitty can snack, but it's best to talk to your own vet. We've said it before, but it's so important we'll say it again: Cats should always have a bowl of clean, fresh water.

5. LITTER BOX LOWDOWN

Kittens learn to use the litter box by copying their mother, so most kittens will already be litter-trained by the time they come home with you. But a new environment with an unfamiliar box and litter can be confusing, so it's a good idea to help your kitty figure things out by placing him in the litter box after he eats and drinks. Start out with a low-sided litter box made especially for kittens, so that they can easily step inside.

6. VET VISITS

The vet should be the very first place your new friend visits. If you don't already have a vet, try asking friends, the local groomer, shelter workers, or the neighbor-hood pet store owner for recommendations. The vet will examine your kitten to make she's healthy, vaccinate her to prevent diseases, and answer all your questions about feeding and training.

7. HANDLING KITTY

Most cats don't naturally love being picked up, so it's best to introduce the idea at a young age. Pet and gently pick up your new kitten frequently and reward him with treats so he learns that attention from you is lots of fun. If kitty squirms, let him go. Forcing a cat or kitten to be held may teach him to dislike it. The more time you spend handling your kitten, the more he'll enjoy attention from people when he's grown up.

8. SOCIAL CREATURES

Once your vet says your kitten is free of diseases and parasites, you can let her explore. The more people and pets she visits when she's young, the calmer she'll be in unfamiliar surroundings when she's an adult. Keep visits short, and reward your kitten with lots of treats and attention.

TRAINING YOUR CAT

If you don't think cats can be trained, check the internet. Videos show felines rolling over, jumping through hoops, and high-fiving on command. *But, you might be thinking, my cat Tiger acts like he doesn't even know his name!* **What gives?**

Cats are naturally active, playful creatures. But they're not born to please people like dogs generally are. However, many do love learning tricks for food rewards. Training is a great way to bond with your kitty, and it can help make some experiences—like getting in a carrier to go to the vet—a lot easier. Here's how you start.

TRAINING BASICS

Start by setting yourself up for success. Don't try training a kitten younger than four months: They can't concentrate well enough to learn effectively, and you'll both end up frustrated. Elderly cats may simply not be interested. Active, intelligent cats, like Siamese (p. 138) and Turkish Angoras (p. 248), are easiest to train, but they're not the only cats that can learn tricks.

Food rewards are the best way to train any animal, including cats. Get some high-quality treats that kitty will go crazy for, such as dehydrated shrimp or dried chicken. It's easiest to train animals when they're a little hungry, so do training sessions right before mealtime and break treats into tiny pieces so your cat doesn't fill up. Training sessions should last just one or two minutes so your cat doesn't get bored.

SIMPLE TRICKS

Start with a basic, useful trick. Teaching your cat to come to you when you call is a great one. Standing close to your kitty, call him by his name and the command "come" while holding out a treat where he can see and smell it. When he walks up to you, reward him with the treat and a "Good kitty!"

Next, try the same thing again, but this time, take a step backward when your cat starts approaching you. Repeat this, each time increasing the distance. After a few sessions, your cat will run to you from another room when called.

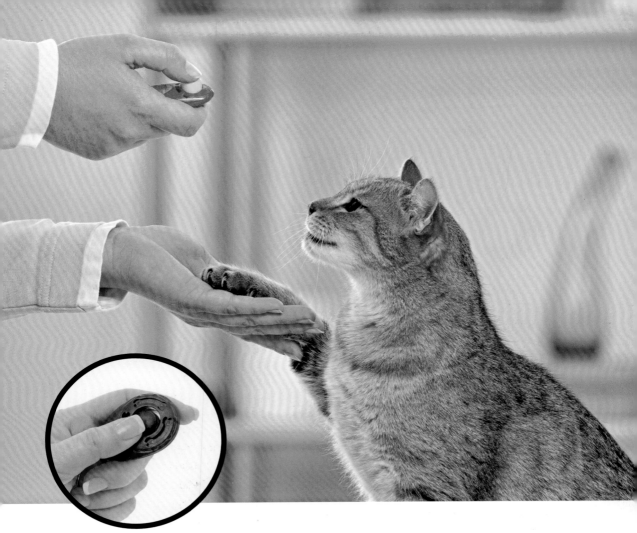

CLICKER TRAINING

For more advanced tricks, clicker training is the way to go. A clicker is a small device with a button that makes a clicking noise when pressed. Clicker training means using the clicker to signal when your cat does the right behavior, then rewarding with a treat. Cats quickly learn that a "click" means a treat is on the way.

Start by teaching your cat to associate the sound of the clicker and a tasty reward. When you have your cat's attention, click and then immediately reward with a treat. Repeat until you notice your cat looking for a treat when he hears the noise.

Now, you're ready to teach a trick. If you want to teach your cat to get in his carrier on command, put your cat near his carrier and say "Inside!" The second your cat looks in the carrier's direction, click and treat. When your cat has that down, start clicking and treating only when he takes a step toward the carrier—then two steps, then when he puts his head inside, and finally, when his whole body is inside. By breaking down behaviors into small steps, then rewarding your cat when he does each one at your command, you can teach all kinds of behaviors.

INDOOR VS. OUTDOOR

Cats love adventure. Curious and independent by nature, they enjoy exploring. But letting your cat roam outside exposes him to dangers such as cars and predators. Read up on the outdoor vs. indoor lifestyle, and choose the one that's right for you and your cat.

CALL OF THE WILD

Cats haven't changed much since their days as wild creatures, when they had no human homes to shelter in. But the world has changed. On top of the predators cats have always had to watch for, like coyotes and birds of prey, many of today's outdoor kitties live in cities and suburbs, where there are lots of busy roads, cars, and other animals. Domestic cats aren't adapted to deal with all of these dangers.

One thing to consider when deciding if you'll let your cat roam outside is her personality. While a calm cat might have no problem spending a lifetime inside, a highly active one might be miserable. Confining an active cat can lead to behavior problems, destroyed furniture, and lots of yowling.

If you are going to let your cat outside, do what you can to lessen the risk. Buy your cat a reflective collar that will help drivers spot and avoid her—and attach a bell to keep your neighborhood's birds safe. Make sure the collar is a "breakaway" type so it will snap off if she gets it caught on a branch. It's safest to make sure your cat is indoors at peak traffic hours and when predators are most active—generally at dawn and dusk. Better yet, train your cat to walk outside on a leash so that you can be with her whenever she's out there. Whether or not you end up letting your cat prowl her outside domain, make sure she has a microchip to identify her if she ever gets lost.

COMFORTS OF HOME

Keeping your cat indoors will mean a much safer—and likely longer—life for your furry friend. If you choose to make your cat an indoor creature, it's your responsibility to help keep her safe, active, and happy.

The first step is making sure your home is free of hazards. Never leave anything unattended that your cat could knock over or harm herself with—such as irons, lit stove burners, or kitchen knives. Watch out for pieces of thread, especially threaded needles, which can harm your cat if swallowed.

Keep cleaners and other chemicals in a place where your cat can't access them. And make sure your houseplants aren't toxic to cats if eaten.

Since your cat can't run and roam to get her energy out, it's up to you to make sure she stays active and doesn't become bored and unhappy. Play with your cat often. If you live in an apartment building, try letting her run around the halls with you along to supervise. (Be sure to check with building management first.) If you have a porch or patio, consider screening it off to give her a little taste of the outdoors.

MISBEHAVIORS

Sometimes, even the sweetest kitty can act up. When behaviors like scratching furniture, litter box problems, or aggression happen, cat owners need to investigate. Often, by finding the source of the problem and using a little patience, these kitty misbehaviors can be minimized or ended entirely.

AGGRESSION

Your cat needs to be taught from the start that behaviors like scratching and biting are unacceptable. If your cat starts acting aggressive while you're playing, it's probably because he's overexcited or because he doesn't want you to touch a sensitive spot like his belly. Nip the behavior in the bud by ending the game immediately and walking away. Don't play too roughly with your cat or use your hands as toys for him to bat at—this can encourage aggressive behavior. And never slap or otherwise physically reprimand a pet: That usually makes the problem worse.

If your cat lashes out at you for what seems like no reason, he may be in pain. Take him to the vet to have him checked out for health problems.

SCRATCHING THE FURNITURE

Scratching is a natural behavior that cats use to sharpen their claws and mark their territory. They don't understand why you wouldn't want them to use your expensive couch for this purpose, and most cats don't learn that your yelling means "Stop!" Try redirecting your cat's claws to a scratching post. Cats usually prefer sturdy, tall posts, but if your cat scratches the carpet, try a horizontal scratching mat instead.

Start by placing the new scratching post right next to the furniture your cat likes to claw. You can cover his old favorite spots on your couch with aluminum foil or double-sided tape to discourage him, and put some catnip inside the post to entice him to the new spot instead. If you want the post out of sight, move it gradually to its permanent location.

SPRAYING

Spraying is how cats mark their territory. Most neutered cats don't spray, but they may start if there is a change to their environment, like a new house, a new baby, or a new pet. Discourage spraying by covering spots he likes to mark with aluminum foil and placing your cat's food nearby. Use safe cleaners designed for households with pets.

LITTER BOX PROBLEMS

Cats love keeping clean, so if you don't clean the litter box regularly, your cat might find somewhere else to go. Scoop it every day, and about once a week, dump all the litter out and give the inside of the box a good cleaning with a pet-safe product. Use an uncovered litter box instead of one with a lid; cats strongly prefer them.

Cats may also avoid the litter box if they experience pain when relieving themselves, because they associate the box with the pain. Take your cat to the vet to make sure an underlying health problem isn't causing the problem.

EATING ISSUES

If your cat bats his food out of his dish before eating it, or doesn't seem to want to eat at all, the problem might be something called whisker fatigue. Some experts think that when cats have to stick their faces inside bowls and their sensitive whiskers rub against the side, the sensation can be stressful. Whisker fatigue is a newly diagnosed condition, and not all vets think it's a real problem. But if your cat is having eating problems, you can try switching to a wide, shallow bowl to see if it helps.

CAT CAREERS

Did this book make you realize you have a passion for cats? If reading about cat evolution, cat breeds, and cat training has inspired you, consider a career that will allow you to spend your days with furry felines. You may need a keep a lint roller with you at all times, but your life is guaranteed to include lots of paw-sitive attention.

1. VETERINARIAN

If your love for Earth's creatures doesn't stop at cats but also includes dogs, guinea pigs, lizards, rabbits, and all other pets, veterinary medicine might be the perfect job for you. Veterinarians and their assistants, veterinary technicians, keep people's beloved pets healthy, heal them when they get sick, and are the first call in emergencies. To be a veterinarian, you'll need to go to college, then be accepted to a four-year veterinary medicine program. Veterinary technicians, who assist the veterinarian, attend a two-year program instead of college (although some go to college first). And if you'd like to specialize in felines, some vets—mostly those in cities—operate cat-only clinics.

2. CAT BEHAVIORIST

Do you feel like you instinctively understand the way a cat's mind works? If so, think about a career as a cat behaviorist. People with this job work with cats and their owners to help solve behavior issues, from the cat that is aggressive toward visitors to the one that's too shy to come out from under the bed. Veterinarians can specialize in feline behavior, but you don't necessarily even need a degree to become a cat behaviorist. Studying something like animal science in school or receiving a certificate from an organization like the International Association of Animal Behavior Consultants will help you become an expert.

3. GROOMER

Even though cats are known for their love of keeping themselves clean and pristine, some occasionally need a little human help. Elderly cats or cats with medical conditions may not be able to bathe themselves very well. And even cats who do keep up on their grooming may develop matted fur that needs professional intervention. Most grooming businesses will train new employees on the job. Organizations like the National Cat Groomers Association of America can help you get started.

5. CAT SITTER

Many cats become anxious when they're away from home. So cat owners are increasingly turning to cat sitters to take care of their beloved pets while they're away. Sometimes, cat sitters stay in the owner's home; other times they stop by once or twice a day to put out food and water, clean the litter box, and give the kitty a little attention. You don't need special training to become a cat sitter, although it's a good idea to get training in animal first aid. The best part about this career is that you can start right away! With your parent's or guardian's permission, offer to watch your friends' or neighbors' cats when they go on vacation. You can also join an association like the National Association of Professional Pet Sitters to help get the word out.

4. BREEDER

Cat breeding often costs more than it pays, so consider it a hobby, not a career. But if you're truly passionate about a particular breed, becoming a professional breeder can give you a way to surround yourself with your favorite kitties. Breeders have to study up on genetics, feline management, and the standards of their chosen breed. Most experts say the best way to get started is to attend cat shows. Watch, learn, and speak with breeders to get their advice and tips.

GLOSSARY

CARNIVORE
an animal that eats meat

CHIMERA
an organism that contains at least two different sets of DNA

CHROMOSOMES
threadlike structures in a cell made of DNA

DNA
deoxyribonucleic acid; a material in a cell that carries information about how a living thing will look and function

DNA SEQUENCING
a process that determines the order of building blocks that make up DNA

DOMINANT GENE
a gene that produces a trait even if it was only passed on by one parent

FERAL
wild

FOUNDER EFFECT
the loss of genetic variation that occurs when a small group of individuals form a new, isolated population

HETEROCHROMIA
being different in color; usually referring to the eyes

HYBRID
the offspring of two different species

MUTATION
a mistake or change in a living thing's DNA

NEURONS
brain cells

POLYDACTYL
a creature that has more than the usual number of toes

RECESSIVE GENE
a gene that only produces a trait if it is passed on by both parents

RIGHTING REFLEX
a reflex that brings a creature's body into normal orientation in space

RUFF
the fur around a cat's neck

SCAVENGER
an animal that feeds on dead animal and plant material

TAPETUM LUCIDUM
a reflective layer in the eye that increases the amount of light for night vision

VIBRISSAE
the long, stiff hairs that grow around the mouths of some mammals, used as touch organs

VOMERONASAL ORGAN
an organ present in some animals that senses smells

FIND OUT MORE

BOOKS

Carney, Elizabeth. *Everything Big Cats.* National Geographic Kids Books, 2011.

Edney, Andrew, and Bruce Fogle. *The Complete Cat Care Manual.* DK, 2006.

Newman, Aline Alexander. *Cat Tales: True Stories of Kindness and Companionship with Kitties.* National Geographic Kids Books, 2017.

Newman, Aline Alexander and Gary Weitzman. *How to Speak Cat: A Guide to Decoding Cat Language.* National Geographic Kids Books, 2015.

The Cat Encyclopedia. DK, 2014.

WEBSITES

Animal Planet's Cats Guide:
animalplanet.com/pets/cats/

The Cat Fanciers' Association:
cfa.org

The International Cat Association:
tica.org

INDEX

Boldface indicates illustrations. If illustrations are included within a page span, the entire span is **boldface**.

PHOTO CREDITS

Abbreviations: AL = Alamy Stock Photo; GI = Getty Images; MP = Minden Pictures; SS = Shutterstock

Cover (feathers), Watcha/GI; (Persian), totojang1977/SS; (British), Photocreo Michal Bednarek/SS; (LO RT), Eric Isselee/SS; (mouse), AnthonyRosenberg/GI; (ball), Suphansa/GI; (LO LE), Ermolaev Alexander/SS; (kitten), Gonalo Barriga/GI; (brush), ra3rn/SS; (UP LE), Idamini/AL; back cover (UP RT), GlobalP/GI; (LO RT), Dave King/GI; (LO LE), 101cats/GI; (ball), Dmitrij Skorobogatov/SS (CTR LE), Eric Isselee/SS; (UP LE), Yellow Cat/SS; spine, Eric Isselee/SS; 1, Okssi/SS; 2, Louno Morose/SS; 3, Utekhina Anna/SS; 4, Andrey_Kuzmin/SS; 5, Chris Winsor/GI; 5, fur texture throughout, Asperger_Syndrome/SS; 6 (LE), San Diego Humane Society; 6 (RT), Life On White/GI; 7, San Diego Humane Society; 9, Jiri Foltyn/SS; 10-11, petographer/AL; 10 (CTR LE), Dave King/Dorling Kindersley/GI; 10 (CTR RT), Marc Henrie/GI; 10 (LO LE), Lux Blue/SS; 11 (LO LE), Jagodka/SS; 11 (LO RT), schankz/SS; 12, cat icon throughout: Hein Nouwens/SS; 12, BirdImages/GI; 13 (UP RT), Red Squirrel/SS; 13 (panthera), Sarah Cheriton-Jones/SS; 13 (CTR RT), Volodymyr Burdiak/SS; 13 (CTR LE), Arno van Dulmen/SS; 13 (LO RT), Helen E. Grose/Dreamstime; 14, GreenArt/SS; 15, Eric Isselee/SS; 16, Sergey Zaykov/SS; 17, Photocreo Michal Bednarek/SS; 18, Yakovlev Sergey/SS; 20, Jon Freeman/AL; 21, Isle of Man/AL; 22 (LE), Lux Blue/SS; 22 (CTR), Jobrestful/GI; 22 (RT), Hilary Andrews/NG Staff; 23 (UP LE), photosounds/SS; 23 (UP RT), Fiona Ayerst/GI; 23 (LO CTR), Michael Duva/GI; 24 (UP LE), Paul Brighton/GI; 24 (UP RT), Life On White/AL; 24 (LO LE), Dave King/GI; 25 (UP LE), Oksana Kuzmina/SS; 25 (LO RT), Sheila Fitzgerald/SS26-27, Chris Winsor/GI; 28, Oksana Bystritskaya/SS; 29, cynoclub/GI; 30, Igor Zhorov/AL; 31, Lavrsen/SS; 32, Kucher Serhii/SS; 33, Konovalov Yevhenii/SS; 34-35, Paisit Teeraphatsakool/SS; 35, Puripat Lertpunyaroj/SS; 36, Chanan Photography/Kimball Stock; 38, pio3/SS; 39 (ears), Pascal Preti/GI; 39 (eyes), Dmitry Naumov/SS; 39 (nose), Steve Gorton and Tim Ridley/GI; 39 (whiskers), fantom_rd/SS; 39 (LO RT), Andrey Ganysh/Dreamstime; 40, krblokhin/GI; 41 (UP RT), Laurie O'Keefe/Science Source; 41 (LO LE), Catchlight Visual Services/AL; 42-43, Robert Fox Photography; 44, Runa Kazakova/SS; 45, Kirill Vorobyev/SS; 46, Koljorova/SS; 47, master1305/GI; 48, Kucher Serhii/SS; 49, petographer/AL; 50, Photocreo Michal Bednarek/SS; 51, Paul_Brighton/GI; 52, Karol Zieli ski/AL; 53, dongshan chen/AL; 54 (UP RT), John Daniels/ARDEA; 54 (LO LE), Anton Balazh/SS; 55 (UP RT), Tony Campbell/SS; 55 (ball), FrankvandenBergh/GI; 55 (LO LE), Tony Campbell/SS; 56-57, Juniors Bildarchiv GmbH/AL; 57 (LO), SNC Art and More/SS; 58, Peter Anderson/AL; 59, petographer/AL; 60, jennybonner/GI; 61, Alan Robinson/AL; 62-63, Labat-Rouquette/Kimball Stock; 64, Sergey Taran/AL; 65, Tatiane Noviski Fornel/GI; 66-67, Jean-Michel Labat/ARDEA; 68, wildcat78/GI; 69, Eric Isselee/SS; 70, Jean-Michel Labat/ARDEA; 71, mdmmikle/SS; 72, Dmitry Galaganov/SS; 73, Labat-Rouquette/Kimball Stock; 74, Labat-Rouquette/Kimball Stock; 75, imageBROKER/AL; 76, aSuruwataRi/SS; 77 (UP LE), Amanda Lewis/GI; 77 (CTR LE), Andrea Izzotti/SS; 77 (RT), History and Art Collection/AL; 78, Ermolaev Alexander/SS; 79 (UP RT), Tsekhmister/SS; 79 (CTR LE), Ahmad Hairi Mohamed/EyeEm/GI; 79 (LO RT), dien/SS; 80-81, jkitan/GI; 81, studiovin/SS; 82, Lebrecht Music & Arts/AL; 83 (UP), Chronicle/AL; 83 (LO), Darla Hallmark/AL; 84, ANCH/SS; 85, Jean-Michel Labat/ARDEA; 86, ewastudio/GI; 87, Vladislav Noseek/SS; 88, Labat-Rouquette/Kimball Stock; 89, Eric Isselee/SS; 90, dien/SS; 91, Yann Arthus-bertrand/ARDEA; 92, Alon Othnay/SS; 93 (UP LE), Viorel Sima/SS; 93 (LO RT), Stiglincz Gabor/SS; 93 (LO), Keisuke_N/SS; 94, Naenaejung/GI; 95, Jean-Michel Labat/GI; 96, Klein-Hubert/Kimball Stock; 97, John Daniels/ARDEA; 98, Life on white/AL; 99, Tierfotoagentur/AL; 100, Tierfotoagentur/AL; 101, Krister Parmstrand/EyeEm/GI; 102, Walt Disney Pictures/courtesy Everett Collection; 103 (UP LE), Warner Bros./Photofest; 103 (UP CTR), © Buena Vista/courtesy Everett Collection; 103 (LO CTR), carlos cardetas/AL; 103 (LO RT), Movie Poster Image Art/GI; 104, Idamini/AL; 104 (UP RT), Juniors Bildarchiv GmbH/AL; 105, Aletakae/GI; 106, NSC Photography/SS; 107, Yann Arthus-bertrand/ARDEA; 108, Idamini/AL; 109 (LE), photo one/SS; 109 (RT), Idamini/AL; 110, Tierfotoagentur/AL; 111, Richard Katris/Chanan Photography; 112, chairboy/GI; 113, Ron Kimball/Kimball Stock; 114, Judith Dzierzawa/Dreamstime; 115, imageBROKER/AL; 116, Dave Watts/MP; 117 (UP LE), Roxana Bashyrova/SS; 117 (UP RT), Arco Images GmbH/AL; 117 (CTR), Olesya Kuznetsova/SS; 117 (LO), vitstudio/SS; 118 (UP), AP Photo/Pat Sullivan; 118 (LO), Photo by Texas A&M University/GI; 119 (UP), Venus the Two Face Cat; 119 (LO RT), virgonira/GI; 119 (LO LE), georgeolsson/GI; 120, Vasiliy Koval/SS; 121, Seregraff/SS; 122, Richard Katris/Chanan Photography; 123, petographer/AL; 124, Utekhina Anna/SS; 125, Krissi Lundgren/SS; 126, Juniors Bildarchiv GmbH/AL; 127, Jean-Michel Labat/ARDEA; 128, Life on white/AL; 129, mdmmikle/SS; 130, GlobalP/GI; 130 (INSET), Nico De Pasquale Photography/GI; 131, Aflo Co., Ltd./AL; 132, Oksana Kuzmina/AL; 133, alexavol/SS; 134, Caters News Agency; 135 (UP LE), BNPS.co.uk; 135 (CTR), Craig Armstrong; 135 (LO), AP Photo/The Tri-City Herald, Paul T. Erickson; 136, Eric Isselee/SS; 137, Eric Isselee/SS; 138-139, Serge75/SS; 140, Steve Prezant/GI; 141, Evgeny Karandaev/AL; 142, Krissi Lundgren/SS; 143, Labat-Rouquette/Kimball Stock; 144, EVasilieva/SS; 145, Klein-Hubert/Kimball Stock; 146, Hughhamilton/Dreamstime; 147, Linn Currie/SS; 148, Andrea Izzotti/SS; 149, Sam

For Molly, of course —SWD

Since 1888, the National Geographic Society has funded more than 12,000 research, exploration, and preservation projects around the world. The Society receives funds from National Geographic Partners, LLC, funded in part by your purchase. A portion of the proceeds from this book supports this vital work. To learn more, visit natgeo.com/info.

NATIONAL GEOGRAPHIC and Yellow Border Design are trademarks of the National Geographic Society, used under license.

For more information, visit nationalgeographic.com, call 1-800-647-5463, or write to the following address:

National Geographic Partners
1145 17th Street N.W.
Washington, D.C. 20036-4688 U.S.A.

Visit us online at nationalgeographic.com/books

For librarians and teachers: ngchildrensbooks.org

More for kids from National Geographic: natgeokids.com

National Geographic Kids magazine inspires children to explore their world with fun yet educational articles on animals, science, nature, and more. Using fresh storytelling and amazing photography, *Nat Geo Kids* shows kids ages 6 to 14 the fascinating truth about the world—and why they should care. **kids.nationalgeographic.com/subscribe**

For information about special discounts for bulk purchases, please contact National Geographic Books Special Sales: specialsales@natgeo.com

For rights or permissions inquiries, please contact National Geographic Books Subsidiary Rights: bookrights@natgeo.com

Designed by Project Design Company

National Geographic supports K–12 educators with ELA Common Core Resources. Visit natgeoed.org/commoncore for more information.

Library of Congress Cataloging-in-Publication Data
Names: Drimmer, Stephanie Warren, author. | National Geographic Kids (Firm), publisher. | National Geographic Society (U.S.)
Title: Cat breed guide/by Stephanie Drimmer.
Description: Washington, DC : National Geographic Kids, [2019] | Audience: Ages 8-12. | Audience: Grades 4 to 6. | Includes index.
Identifiers: LCCN 2018031439 | ISBN 9781426334399 (hardcover) | ISBN 9781426334405 (hardcover)
Subjects: LCSH: Cat breeds--Juvenile literature. | Cats--Juvenile literature.
Classification: LCC SF445.7 .D74 2019 | DDC 636.8--dc23
LC record available at https://lccn.loc.gov/2018031439

The publisher would like to thank everyone who worked to make this book come together: Stephanie Drimmer, writer; Jen Agresta, project manager; Angela Modany, associate editor; Dr. Gary Weitzman and Mieshelle Nagelschneider, expert reviewers; Sarah J. Mock, senior photo editor; and Sanjida Rashid, art director.

Printed in China
19/RRDS/1